Publish. Promote. Monetize.

How Coaches, Experts, and Thought Leaders Build Authority and a Personal Brand, Grow Their Business, and Turn Their Books into Profit Machines

H.J. Chammas

AUTHORITY
PUBLISHING

1st Edition 2026.

ISBN (Paperback): 978-1-965480-49-6

ISBN (Hardback): 978-1-965480-51-9

ISBN (eBook): 978-1-965480-48-9

Authority Publishing

www.authority-publishing.com

Printed in the United States of America.

Table of content

Dedication   V

Preface   VII

Introduction   1

Part I: Publish   11

1. Step 1: Nail Your Big Idea   13

2. Step 2: Know Your Reader Better Than They Know Themselves   38

3. Step 3: Reverse-Engineer Success   53

4. Step 4: Craft a Book That Sells Itself   66

5. Step 5: Optimize for the Amazon Search Engine   80

6. Step 6: Seed Monetization Inside Your Book   117

Part II: Promote   136

7. Step 7: Optimize Your Amazon Listing Before You Go to Print   139

8. Step 8: Drive Traffic Where It Matters   159

9. Step 9: Turn Visibility Into Credibility   187

10. Step 10: Create Momentum Beyond Launch Day   213

Part III: Monetize   244

11. Step 11: Build Your Author Ecosystem   247

12. Step 12: Design Offers That Scale Your Impact   260

13. Step 13: Fuel the System With Smart Traffic   277

14. Step 14: Turn Your Book Into a Business Growth Engine   292

Conclusion   306

Help Me Help Other Authors   309

About H.J. Chammas   311

Acknowledgements   313

For all the coaches, experts, and consultants out there...
those who are trying hard, hustling every day,
chasing impact, changing lives, and building something that matters.

This book is for you.

For the late nights, the early mornings, the quiet doubts, and the loud
dreams.
For every time you've wondered if all this effort will ever pay off—
keep going. The world needs what you have to give.

And to my son, Ryan—
who's already walking this path at just eight years old.
You remind me every day why this work matters.
Watching you write your own books, edit your stories, design your pages,
and learn the craft from the ground up fills me with pride.
You're not just following in my footsteps; you're carving your own.
I believe you'll grow into a remarkable author one day...
and maybe even a publisher too.

Preface

Let me save you sixty-five thousand dollars.

That's how much I spent to learn how *not* to publish a book.

Back then, I was wide-eyed, excited, and—let's be honest—dangerously optimistic. My first book, *The Employee Millionaire*, was almost done. I had this vision of walking through airports and seeing my name on the shelf next to *Rich Dad Poor Dad*. I was *the next Robert Kiyosaki!* (At least in my head.)

Then came the call that changed everything.
A big-name publishing company's "self-publishing division" said they loved my idea. *"We'll handle everything,"* they promised. *"Editing, cover, distribution, marketing... you'll just sit back and collect royalties."*

It sounded perfect. I was excited... mostly because their logo had a penguin on it... it looks like I made it to the big publisher! I thought, *"If that's on my cover, I've made it."*

They said they had *solutions for authors*. Turns out, the only problem they solved was theirs, not mine.

It sounded like a dream.

It was actually tuition.

They sent me shiny proposals and convincing sales decks with phrases like *"global exposure," "media campaigns,"* and *"exclusive author events."* Somewhere in that pile of excitement and paperwork, I missed the fine print: I wasn't partnering with a publisher. I was *paying* one.

And pay, I did.

Every add-on came with a price tag. *"You'll need the premium marketing package,"* they said. *"This press release distribution will boost your visibility." "These bookstore placements are limited—act fast."*

You know how those all-inclusive vacations never really include every-thing?
Yeah. Like that. But without the beach.

By the time the dust settled, I'd spent $65,000.

And when my royalty statement arrived!
Let's just say it didn't require a calculator.

Less than two thousand dollars in total earnings... in the first two years.

That's when it hit me—*I hadn't paid for a publishing service; I'd paid for a very expensive lesson.*

I wasn't a published author.
I was a published victim.

The dream of seeing my book change lives turned into the nightmare of realizing I'd been sold an illusion.

But looking back now, I wouldn't trade that lesson for anything. Because that painful, humbling, slightly ridiculous chapter is where *Publish Promote Monetize* really began.

From Pain to Publishing Geek

After the $65,000 heartbreak, I did what any rational person would do.

I sulked.
Then I got angry.

Then, one night around 2 a.m., while staring at my sales dashboard like it had personally betrayed me, I made a decision: *"I'm going to figure this out myself."*

No more paid *"marketing packages."* No more *"exclusive visibility campaigns."* No more pretending someone else could care about my book more than I did.

I went down the rabbit hole.

Metadata, keywords, categories, book descriptions, cover design psychology—you name it, I studied it. I devoured everything I could find about how *Amazon*'s algorithm worked. I learned what makes a book clickable, what makes readers stop scrolling, and what makes *Amazon* actually recommend you.

It wasn't glamorous. Picture me hunched over a laptop, surrounded by empty coffee mugs, whispering to myself like a conspiracy theorist.

But it worked.

I republished *The Employee Millionaire*—this time completely under my own control. New title positioning, optimized keywords, targeted categories, and a redesigned cover that didn't scream *"template special."*

And suddenly, things started to move. Sales trickled in. Reviews appeared. Rankings climbed. My book was actually *visible*.

I'd gone from paying someone to *"market"* my book to realizing that if I could learn the system, I could *be* the system.

"This time, I didn't buy a marketing package. I became one."

What started as frustration turned into fascination. I became obsessed with what really makes a book sell—not the hype, not the vanity packages, but the data, psychology, and positioning behind every successful title.

And the best part? I discovered that the difference between a forgotten book and a bestseller wasn't luck. It was a process.

It Wasn't Luck; It Was a System

Once *The Employee Millionaire* took off, I had one question spinning in my head: *"Was this a fluke?"*

So, I ran the experiment again.
Then again.
And again.

Three more books. Three bestsellers. Each one launched differently, but the results were the same: steady rankings, organic sales, and visibility that kept compounding month after month.

That's when I knew... it wasn't luck. It was a system.

The same process worked every time: clear positioning, keyword optimization, professional design, and authentic reviews fueled by a real audience, not friends doing me favors.

I wasn't guessing anymore. I was tracking. Testing. Tweaking.

Every book became a data point, every launch a lab experiment. I saw patterns—what worked universally, what failed spectacularly, and what could be simplified so any author could replicate it.

The more I studied, the more obvious it became: publishing wasn't an art project. It was an ecosystem.

And once you understood that ecosystem, you could build a book that sells itself, without needing to beg for reviews, chase trends, or dump money into social media ads that make more noise than sales. Amazon Ads, though? That's a different story. When used strategically, they're the engine that keeps the book visible to the right readers at the right time.

I remember laughing one night while updating my ad dashboard and whispering to myself, *"I went from publishing victim to publishing nerd faster than Amazon could approve my next ad campaign."*

What started as survival had become science.

I finally had something real... repeatable, measurable, and teachable.

The Accidental Mentor

When something starts working, people notice.

At first, it was just a few authors in my circle asking questions: *"Hey, how did you get your book to rank on Amazon?"* or *"Who's running your ads?"*

Then, strangers started messaging me. Authors I'd never met. Coaches, consultants, experts—people who'd been burned by the same kind of publishing promises I once believed.

The funny thing is, I wasn't even active online. I'm an introvert by nature. I wasn't posting daily selfies or running webinars. I was just quietly doing my thing, experimenting, and refining.

But somehow, word got out.

My *LinkedIn* following grew from under 500 to around 15,000. My *X* (formerly *Twitter*) account crossed 20,000. And these weren't random followers; they were serious authors who'd seen my results and wanted to learn how to do it right.

At first, I helped them for free. I shared templates, checklists, and lessons I'd learned the hard way. I didn't want anyone to go through what I did.

And here's the part that still amazes me: every single author I helped went on to become a bestseller. Every. Single. One.

That's when something clicked.

One day, an author I'd helped messaged me and said, *"You know, H.J., you should really do this as a business."*

I laughed it off at first. Me? Start a publishing company? I had no office, no staff, and no plan.

But the idea wouldn't leave me alone.

The more authors I helped, the more I realized this wasn't just about books. It was about redemption. Turning that painful $65,000 mistake into a system that could save others from making the same one.

I didn't plan to become a mentor. I just wanted to fix my own mess.

But that's the thing about purpose—it usually finds you while you're busy cleaning up your mistakes.

The Birth of Authority Publishing

So I did it. I turned that accidental mentorship into something real.

No fancy investors. No shiny offices. Just a laptop, a coffee mug, and a stubborn belief that authors deserved better.

That's how *Authority Publishing* was born.

The goal was simple: help authors publish, promote, and monetize their books the right way—without the overpriced "packages," the broken promises, or the smoke and mirrors.

In our first year, we published six to eight books. Every single one became a bestseller.

That's when I knew this wasn't luck or coincidence—it was proof of concept.

We took the same system I had refined over my own journey and built it into a process any author could follow. A process that wasn't about hype, but about *positioning*. Not about chasing algorithms, but about understanding them.

Three years later, we'd published more than fifty books. Each one had its own story, its own message, and its own audience—but the results were the same. Consistent visibility. Real readers. Sustainable momentum.

That's what makes me proudest.
We don't do one-day *Kindle* fame. We build the *"forever"* kind of success.

When other publishers were bragging about temporary spikes, we were helping authors create long-term authority: books that stayed relevant, ranked organically, and turned into businesses.

Because that's the real game. Publishing isn't about selling a book; it's about building everything that comes after it.

And the best part? Watching authors realize that for the first time, seeing that lightbulb moment when they go, *"Wait, this isn't just about a book... this is about building something bigger."*

That's when I knew we weren't just publishing books anymore.

We were building legacies.

The Fiction Detour (The Funny Lesson)

Before *Authority Publishing* found its rhythm, I decided to experiment.

I thought, *"Hey, if we can make non-fiction books successful, imagine what we can do with fiction!"*

Spoiler: we imagined wrong.

The fiction world was a different beast altogether. No clear niches. No business ecosystem. No built-in offers beyond... well, book royalties.

And royalties, I quickly learned, are not a business model.

We poured energy into brilliant covers, catchy blurbs, and clever ads. But unless you already had a loyal fan base or were willing to spend like a Hollywood studio, it was like shouting into a hurricane.

The competition was brutal. Thousands of new fiction titles are released every day. Beautiful stories buried under an avalanche of equally beautiful stories.

I remember thinking, *"So this is what it feels like to play roulette with your wallet."*

That's when it hit me: fiction is like gambling in *Las Vegas*. Non-fiction, on the other hand, is like owning the casino.

When you write a non-fiction book, you're not relying on royalties to survive. You're building authority, credibility, and trust. Your book becomes the front door to your business, not the end of it.

In fiction, the book *is* the product. In non-fiction, the book *creates* the product.

That's when our focus became crystal clear.

We stopped chasing genres and started building authority ecosystems—books designed to elevate experts, coaches, and consultants who had something real to teach.

And from that moment on, everything we did had one goal: help authors turn their ideas into impact and their stories into systems.

The Hidden Struggle Every Expert Faces

Most coaches, consultants, and experts aren't struggling because they lack skill; they're struggling because they lack *trust*.

You can post every day on *LinkedIn*, record Reels on *Instagram*, or share insights on X. You might even get engagement. But when it comes time for clients to decide—to actually hire you—something still hesitates inside them.

Are they the real deal?

Can I trust them?

Or are they just another fly-by-night expert with polished words and no proof?

That invisible question is what stops conversions long before a sales call begins.

Extroverts sometimes get through it with charm. But most experts—especially the thoughtful, introverted ones—find it exhausting to constantly "perform" credibility.

That's why a book changes everything.

When you publish a book, you're no longer just *telling* people what you know; you're *showing* it. You've taken the time to organize your ideas, articulate your frameworks, and put your thinking on record.
It's proof of depth, and it builds trust faster than any post, video, or ad campaign ever could.

Now, stack that trust.
Your book gets nominated for an award... credibility rises.
Readers leave reviews... social proof multiplies.
Editorial mentions appear... authority expands.
The book climbs bestseller lists... perception transforms.

Suddenly, you're not just a coach or consultant. You're an *award-winning, bestselling author* who also happens to coach, consult, or advise. And that one distinction reshapes how the market sees you.

> *Clients don't just buy your service; they buy certainty.*
> *And nothing communicates certainty quite like am award-winning bestselling book that bears your name.*

The Bigger Message

After all the trial, error, and late-night Amazon rabbit holes, one truth became impossible to ignore.

Most authors chase the wrong goal.

They obsess over sales charts, royalty dashboards, and launch day screenshots. But here's the real secret:

The goal isn't to sell the book; it's to build what the book sells.

A book is not the business. It's the bridge.

That bridge can lead to clients, courses, speaking opportunities, partnerships, or entire movements. But it only works if you build it with purpose.

That's what *Publish Promote Monetize* is about.

It's not another feel-good publishing pep talk or a "How I did it" memoir. It's a roadmap for authors who want results that actually pay off.

Because the truth is, you don't need a viral post or a million followers to build a thriving author brand. You just need a clear message, a focused niche, and a system that turns readers into relationships.

And that system works... again and again.

After my first failure, I applied it to my next books. Two of them have each sold more than one hundred thousand copies. Not because of luck. Not because of a big publisher's marketing machine. But because the process worked... and I stayed patient enough to play the long game.

It's proof that success in publishing doesn't come from chasing spikes; it comes from building momentum that lasts.

The *Publish Promote Monetize* system starts where most authors stop—on *Amazon,* the world's largest bookstore. But it doesn't end there. Once your foundation is strong, you expand to every major retailer and eventually into global bookstore distribution. That's how authority scales beyond a single platform.

This isn't about chasing trends or gaming algorithms. It's about building authority that compounds over time by publishing strategically, promoting smartly, and monetizing intentionally.

And yes, it takes patience. You'll test, adjust, and learn from your audience. Some things will flop. Others will surprise you. That's the beauty of it—it's not instant fame. It's sustainable growth.

If you stick with it, if you learn to see your book not as an end but as a beginning, you'll build something that outlasts the hype.

This book is everything I wish someone had handed me before I made that $65,000 mistake.

At the end of the day, a book isn't just something you sell; it's something that sells you.

If you're holding this book right now, you're already ahead of where I was when I started. You haven't spent $65,000 yet, and you don't need to.

All you need is clarity—on your message, your audience, and the purpose behind your book.

Because once you see publishing for what it really is—a credibility engine, not a lottery ticket—everything changes.

You'll stop chasing *"bestseller"* banners and start building an ecosystem that feeds your authority long after launch day.

So take a deep breath, grab a coffee, and get ready to rethink everything you've been told about books, marketing, and monetization.

This is where your story as an *authority author* begins.

Introduction

The Myth of the "Finished Book"

You know that feeling when you finally hit *publish*? The rush, the pride, the "I did it!" moment. You've poured your heart, your time, and your caffeine supply into this thing... and now it's out there. You've crossed the finish line.

Except... you haven't.

Most authors think *publishing* is the end of the marathon when it's actually the starting line. They celebrate with champagne, post the *"It's out!"* update, and then wait.

And wait.

When nothing happens—no sales, no buzz, no *"Congrats, I saw your book everywhere!"*—they start wondering what went wrong.

Wasn't this supposed to change everything?

Here's the hard truth: writing and publishing your book is only 10% of the journey. The other 90% is making sure people actually find it, read it, and connect it back to *you* and your brand.

Because the book itself isn't the goal; it's the doorway.

What most people call "publishing a book" is really just *making it available.* That's like opening a restaurant and forgetting to tell anyone where it is. You've cooked the meal, but unless you've invited the guests, nobody's showing up.

That's where so many smart, talented authors stumble. They think the finish line is a product when it's really a platform.

What if your book isn't the end product, but the beginning of your authority?

When you treat your book like a business tool instead of a personal milestone, everything changes. The focus shifts from *"I published a book"* to *"I built a brand."* From *"I got my message out"* to *"I positioned myself as the go-to authority in my niche."*

Publishing isn't the reward for writing; it's the ignition switch for what comes next.

Visibility Isn't the Same as Credibility

You can be everywhere online and still feel invisible where it matters most: in the mind of your ideal client. You post, share insights, and maybe even go live once in a while. But when the moment of truth comes, when a potential client asks themselves, *"Should I trust this person?"*, there's still hesitation.

That's not because you lack skill. It's because you lack proof.

Visibility might get you attention, but only credibility earns trust. And trust is the real currency of conversion.

That's where your book changes everything.

A book bridges that credibility gap faster than anything else. It says, *"I've organized my ideas, refined my thinking, and put my expertise into something tangible."* It's not another passing post or recycled carousel; it's your knowledge, documented. And that changes how people see you.

Suddenly, you're not just another expert with a service. You're an award-winning author with a framework people believe in.

That's the real game. Not chasing followers or likes, but building trust that compounds with every page, every review, and every reader who sees your name in print.

Your book doesn't just tell people what you do. It proves who you are.

> *What would your business look like if clients trusted you before you ever met them?*
> That's what publishing your book strategically makes possible.

Why Most Books Fail (and Why It's Not Your Fault)

Let's get this out of the way: if your book didn't sell, it's probably not because you're a bad writer.

Most books fail because their authors were sold the wrong game.

They were told to focus on writing and "getting published," not on positioning, visibility, or monetization. They were told that once the book is live on *Amazon*, the world would magically discover it. *Spoiler: it doesn't.*

The truth is, the old publishing system was never designed to help authors succeed; it was designed to make publishers money. And the self-publishing world? It copied the same habits, only with prettier dashboards.

You've probably seen the same promises I did: *"We'll handle everything: editing, cover design, distribution, printing!"* You sign the check, they hand you a copy of your book, and that's where the relationship ends.

No marketing strategy. No data. No understanding of keywords, categories, or audience behavior.

You're left holding a beautiful book that no one knows exists.

It's not your fault. You were told to write the book you wanted to write, not the one your readers were searching for.

Think about that for a second.

You can write the most insightful, life-changing book in your niche, but if nobody can find it, you've built a billboard in the middle of the desert.

Here's the good news: the problem isn't your book. It's the system.

The system rewards visibility, not value. It prioritizes metadata over message. It pushes authors to "launch" instead of position.

But once you understand how the game is really played—how Amazon's search engine works, how readers discover books, and how to align your message with your market—you stop being a passenger in your own publishing journey.

You start driving.

And that's what this book is about. It's not about writing faster or spending more on ads. It's about learning to publish strategically, promote intelligently, and monetize sustainably.

Once you master that, you're no longer hoping your book works.
You're engineering it to work.

The New Game: Authority Publishing

If you've ever watched a first-time author hit *publish*, you know the look: equal parts excitement and mild panic. It's that moment when they realize, *Wait... now what?*

That's where the new game begins.

Traditional publishing tells you to think like an author: write a great book, hope someone notices, and move on to the next one.
But *Authority Publishing* flips that mindset. It invites you to think like an entrepreneur: create value, own your message, and let the book become a cornerstone of something bigger.

It's not about selling books; it's about building an ecosystem around what the book represents.

In this new game, your book isn't the product; you are. The book is simply the proof.

Think of it as your business card with staying power. When someone hands you a business card, you might smile, nod, and forget it by the next meeting. But when someone gives you a book, you pause. You hold it. You flip through the pages. You instantly sense credibility, effort, and expertise.

A book says, *"I know what I'm talking about."* It opens doors, starts conversations, and builds trust before you ever speak a word.

The difference between authors who struggle and those who thrive isn't luck. It's understanding how to turn a book into leverage.

Because the game has changed. The most successful authors today aren't chasing followers, bestseller banners, or one-day spikes. They're building lasting visibility, authority, and trust... one reader at a time.

That's what *Authority Publishing* is all about. It's a long-term mindset that connects your message to the people who need it most and helps your book keep working for you long after launch day.

Your book becomes more than a project; it becomes a platform.
More than a milestone, it becomes momentum.
And once you start playing that game, the old way of publishing will feel like trying to win a championship with a broken playbook.

What This Book Will Teach You

So, what are we actually doing here?

This isn't another *"how to self-publish"* manual that leaves you stranded once your book goes live. You don't need another checklist or tutorial. You need a clear system: a practical, step-by-step way to turn your book into lasting credibility, meaningful reach, and consistent opportunities.

That's what this book is designed to give you.

We'll start by fixing the foundation: how to *publish strategically* so your book is discoverable, competitive, and positioned for success from day one. You'll learn how to identify your Big Idea, understand your readers, and shape your book to meet a real need in the market.

Then we'll move to the next phase: how to *promote effectively*. You'll see how discoverability works on *Amazon*, what truly influences reviews and rankings, and how to create visibility that doesn't fade after launch week.

Finally, we'll bring it all together with the third phase: how to *monetize intelligently*. Because the real power of a book isn't in royalties; it's in the doors it opens. Speaking engagements, consulting opportunities, online programs, collaborations... your book can become the entry point to all of them.

By the end, you'll have a repeatable process to launch, grow, and sustain a book that not only sells but also serves.

No hype. No gimmicks. Just timeless principles, clear direction, and lessons that work whether you're writing your first book or scaling your author platform.

Once you understand how publishing, promotion, and monetization fit together, you'll never look at your book—or your business—the same way again.

Your Commitment

Before we dive in, make a small promise to yourself, not to me.

Promise that you'll stop treating your book like a product and start treating it like a platform.

Because from this point on, everything changes.

This isn't about chasing bestseller badges or posting screenshots of rankings on *Amazon*. It's about building something that lasts. Something that opens doors, builds trust, and positions you as a steady voice in your field.

If you're willing to think differently and play the long game, this book will show you how.

You'll see that real success in publishing has nothing to do with luck. It's about alignment: the right book, for the right reader, with the right plan behind it.

That's the heart of the *Publish, Promote, Monetize* framework. It's not theory; it's a way of thinking that helps your book serve a larger purpose.

But it all starts with commitment.

The commitment to stop hoping and start engineering your success.

To stop asking, *"Will my book work?"* and start asking, *"How can I make it work for me?"*

As you read on, remember this: you're not just publishing a book. You're shaping your brand, expanding your reach, and building something that can outlast you.

That journey begins here... by getting the foundation right.

Publishing isn't just about putting words on paper; it's about positioning those words to make an impact.

A Note Before We Begin

In this book, you'll learn the *how-to*—the strategies, frameworks, and timeless principles that make your book work for you. You'll understand not just *what* to do, but *why* it matters and *how* it fits into your larger business ecosystem.

What you won't find here are endorsements for specific technologies, paid tools, or platforms—and that's intentional.
Technology evolves. Algorithms shift. Interfaces change. But strategy—the art of positioning, promoting, and monetizing your book with purpose—never goes out of date.

This book is meant to be evergreen. The principles inside have worked for years, across markets and platforms, and they'll keep working long after the next update or trend fades.
Yes, you'll see mentions, but only as examples of how timeless strategy shows up in the real world, not as recommendations of what you *must* use.

So as you read, focus on what endures: understanding your reader, crafting your message, positioning your book, and building trust that compounds over time. Because when you master that, the tools will always serve you—not the other way around.

In *Part I*, we'll explore how to publish strategically: how to define your *Big Idea*, understand your reader, and shape your book into an authority-building asset rather than just a creative project.

By the time you finish this section, you won't just know how to write a book. You'll know how to build one that connects, sells, and opens doors long after launch day.

Part I: Publish
Your Book Is the Beginning of Your Authority

You've seen why publishing isn't the finish line; it's the foundation.

This is where your journey as an *authority author* really begins.

Because at this stage, your goal isn't just to *write* a book. It's to build one that works.
One that opens doors, builds credibility, and positions you as the trusted voice in your space.

Publishing isn't about putting words on paper. It's about placing your name in the conversation that matters most... the one happening inside your reader's mind.
When done right, your book doesn't just tell your story; it starts theirs.

This is where you stop thinking like an author and start thinking like an architect. You're designing the foundation of an ecosystem: one that connects your message, your market, and your mission.

Over the next six steps, we'll break down exactly how to publish like an authority, not an amateur. You'll learn how to:

1. Nail your Big Idea so your book becomes a bridge between what you *know* and what your readers *need*.

2. Understand your audience so deeply that every page feels written just for them.

3. Reverse-engineer success by studying what already works in your market.

4. Craft a book that sells itself through clarity, not hype.

5. Optimize your presence on *Amazon* and other book retailers so the right readers find you.

6. Seed monetization inside your book so it naturally drives leads, clients, and opportunities.

Think of this part as your launchpad: the point where ideas become impact.
Because when your book is built with strategy, every word you publish becomes a stepping stone toward visibility, credibility, and long-term profit.

Ready to build the kind of book that changes everything?

Let's start with Step 1: *Nail Your Big Idea.*

Step 1: Nail Your Big Idea

Clarity Creates Credibility

Before you publish anything, before you hire an editor, design a cover, or even choose a title, you need to answer one question: *What game are you actually playing?*

The difference between a book that drives your business forward and one that disappears into Amazon's black hole almost always comes down to one thing: *clarity*.

Clarity about who you are, what you stand for, and who your book is meant to serve.

You've already seen in the Preface and Introduction how a book transforms perception and bridges the credibility gap between visibility and trust. Now it's time to make sure you're building the right book to carry that trust.

The wrong idea, even beautifully published, can't create authority. But the right idea, when it aligns with your mission, your reader, and your business, becomes unstoppable.

That's what this first step is about.

Not writing faster or publishing sooner, but building the foundation that makes every future success possible: clarity.

Once you've nailed your Big Idea, everything else—your message, your promotion, and your monetization—begins to align naturally.

Stop Thinking Like an Author; Start Thinking Like an Authority

Most people start their book the same way: staring at a blank page and asking themselves, *"What do I want to say?"*

That's the first mistake.

Because here's the truth. Nobody's waiting to hear what you want to say. They're waiting to hear what they need to hear.

That one shift changes everything.

It's the difference between writing a book that fades away and one that builds momentum for your business.
Between publishing a personal project and positioning yourself as the go-to expert in your space.

This is where most well-meaning authors go wrong. They treat their book like a diary instead of a direction. They pour in their stories, their lessons, their "aha" moments… and then wonder why the book doesn't sell or lead anywhere.

But your book isn't supposed to be your life story. It's supposed to be your reader's shortcut.

Your reader doesn't want to read about how you climbed the mountain. They want you to hand them the map so they can start their own climb.

That's what it means to think like an authority.

An authority doesn't write to impress. They write to instruct, to guide, and to solve. They understand that their story is the proof, not the point.

So if you've been thinking about your book as a way to "share what's inside you," that's fine, but it's not enough. Authority doesn't come from what's inside you. It comes from how well you can draw out what's inside someone else.

Let's be honest. Every market today is flooded with noise. Everyone's posting, publishing, and promising. The difference between another "book on a topic" and a book that builds trust is focus.

And focus starts here. Not with what you want to say, but with what your reader desperately needs to hear.

So let's flip the script.

Instead of asking, *"What do I want to tell the world?"* ask yourself:
"What does my ideal reader wake up worrying about?"
"What's the pain they can't solve, the question they keep Googling, the frustration that keeps them stuck?"

That's where your book begins.

When you start with your reader, your message naturally finds its mission. You stop writing from opinion and start writing from purpose.

And when your purpose aligns with your expertise, everything changes. Your book stops being another personal project and becomes a positioning asset.

It's no longer just something you wrote. It's proof of what you know, why it matters, and how it helps.

That's when people start seeing you differently. You're not just an author anymore. You're the authority people turn to for answers.

Nail Your Big Why

Before you write a single word, let's talk about something most authors never stop to ask themselves.

Why are you really writing this book?

And no, I don't mean the polished answer you'd post on LinkedIn. I mean the real one: the one that might sound a little selfish, a little scary, or maybe even a little messy.

Because here's the thing. Your *why* shapes every decision that follows. It shapes the kind of book you write, the way you show up to promote it, and how it fits into your bigger business story.

If your *why* is fuzzy, your book will be too.

So let's get it out in the open.

There are five main reasons people write books. You might see yourself in one, two, or even all of them. But one will always lead the way.

1. Impact

You've learned something the hard way, and you don't want others to go through it blind.
You've got lessons that could save people years of trial, error, and frustration.

Your motivation is contribution. You want to make a difference. You want to pass the torch, not keep it to yourself.

That's impact.

2. Legacy

This one goes deeper than business. It's about leaving something that outlives you.
You want your ideas, your message, and your hard-won experience to mean something to your family, your field, or maybe to the next generation of dreamers who'll walk your path.

You're not just writing for readers. You're writing for the record.

That's legacy.

3. Business

You've built something that works—a system, a framework, a way of thinking—and you're ready to scale it.
You're tired of saying the same things on every client call. You want your book to do the talking for you.

In this case, your book isn't just a message. It's a marketing asset.
It opens doors, starts conversations, and builds trust before you ever show up.

That's business.

4. Coaching and Scaling

You love helping people, but there's only one of you.
Writing a book lets you multiply your message without multiplying your hours.

Your book becomes the front door to your coaching, your community, and your movement.
It's how you reach more people without burning out.

That's scaling through service.

5. Ego (and it's okay)

Let's be honest. Some part of you wants to hold your book in your hands, see your name on the cover, and post that "I did it!" photo.

And that's perfectly fine.
There's no shame in wanting recognition. The key is not to stop there.

Ego can light the fire. Just make sure purpose keeps it burning.

You might see yourself in a few of these... and that's normal.

But one of them is your core driver.

If it's *impact*, you'll write with empathy and heart.
If it's *business*, you'll focus on results.
If it's *legacy*, your tone will be more reflective and timeless.

Knowing your *why* keeps you grounded when writing gets hard... and trust me, it will.
It keeps you focused when you start thinking, *"Maybe I should write something for everyone."*

You're not here to write *any* book.
You're here to write the *right* book: one that moves you, serves your reader, and builds your authority all at once.

So before you move on, grab a notebook and finish this sentence:

"I'm writing this book because..."

Don't edit it. Don't overthink it. Just write what's true.

When you know your why, your message gains power.
And when your message has power, your book has purpose.

Your Book Isn't About You; It's About the Problem You Solve

This might sting a little... but it needs to be said.

Your reader isn't here for you; they're here for what you can help them achieve.

Not your story. Not your journey. Not even your *"why."*

What they care about is what your story can do for them.

Every reader opens a book for one reason: they want something. They want to feel different, think differently, or finally fix something that's been bothering them for a long time.

If your book helps them do that, they'll remember you forever. If it doesn't, they'll forget your name by page ten.

And if you're still reading this and you've made it past page ten, congratulations... you're officially more committed than most readers. Keep going; you're my kind of person.

That's the truth.

And it's why your book can't just be a highlight reel of your life or career. It has to be a mirror.

Think about *Rich Dad Poor Dad.*
It didn't succeed because readers cared about Robert Kiyosaki's story; it worked because they saw themselves in it. They recognized their own fears about money, their own limiting beliefs, and their own "poor dad" thinking.

Kiyosaki wasn't the hero. He was the guide.

The story wasn't about him; it was about the reader's transformation.

That's what makes a book powerful.
It stops being about the author and starts being about the audience.

When you shift from *your experience* to *their outcome,* everything changes.
Because authority doesn't come from how much you know; it comes from how well you understand what your audience is going through.

So here's a little reality check.

If your first thought is, *"I just want to tell my story,"* pause for a second and ask yourself, *"Why would someone who's never met me care?"*

Now flip it.
"What result would make my reader thank me when they finish this book?"

That's the shift: from *author* to *authority.*

When you write from empathy instead of ego, your reader feels it.
They stop seeing you as someone talking *at* them and start seeing you as someone who gets them.

And once they trust that you get it, they'll follow you anywhere... into your frameworks, your programs, your services, and even your next book.

Here's the golden rule:

> *You are not the hero of your book. Your reader is.*
> *You're the guide who's been where they are, faced what they fear,*
> *and found the way out.*

That's why your book matters.
Not because of who you are, but because of who it helps them become.

The "Book-Worthy" Idea Test

Let's get something straight. Not every idea deserves a book.

Some ideas are great for blog posts, podcasts, or *LinkedIn* updates that get a few likes and disappear into the feed. But a *book-worthy* idea? That's something else entirely.

A book-worthy idea isn't just something you *want* to say; it's something your audience *needs* to hear right now.
It's the topic that keeps showing up in your conversations, the question your clients keep asking, and the frustration your audience keeps voicing.

That's your Big Idea.

And here's how you know if it's strong enough to turn into a book.

A blog post *shares* an opinion.
A book *shifts* perspective.

A blog post *teaches* something new.
A book *transforms* how people think, act, and make decisions.

A blog post *ends* at the page.
A book *opens* a door to your framework, your method, your business, or your way of solving the problem.

See the difference?

Your Big Idea isn't the one that makes you sound smart.
It's the one that makes your reader say, *"Finally, someone gets it."*

To find that idea, connect three simple dots:

- A clear audience that's already hungry for a solution.

- A painful problem they haven't been able to solve.

- A proven process or perspective that you've lived, tested, or taught.

That's it. You don't need to reinvent the wheel; you just need to explain why your version of the wheel works better.

It all comes down to knowing *why* this message matters... not just to you, but to the people who will read it. Your *why* gives your book weight and meaning. Without it, even the smartest idea falls flat.

So before you rush off brainstorming titles or chapter lists, take a breath and ask yourself three quick questions:

Who exactly is this book for?
What problem are they living with that I can help them solve?
And what do I want them to be able to do differently by the last page?

If you can answer those three questions clearly, congratulations... you don't just have a book idea; you have a business asset in disguise.

A book that's built around one problem, one promise, and one path doesn't just sell copies.

It sells clarity. It builds trust. And it gives your audience a reason to follow you long after they finish reading.

Fit In and Stand Out

Let's clear up a common myth in publishing: *"My book needs to be totally original."*

No, it doesn't.

If nobody's written about your topic before, that's not a green light; it's a red flag. It usually means there's no proven demand.

Every successful book fits into an existing conversation but adds something fresh to it.
That's what I call the Fit In and Stand Out principle.

You want your book to belong on the same shelf as the bestsellers in your niche. Readers should instantly think, *"Ah, this is the kind of book I like."* But then they should feel an immediate pull... *"Wait, this one's different."*

That's how bestsellers are born.

Look at *Atomic Habits.* There were already dozens of habit books out there. But James Clear added his twist: focusing on small improvements that compound over time.
He fit into a crowded niche, then stood out with a fresh lens and a sticky framework.

Or think of *Rich Dad Poor Dad*. It didn't invent personal finance. It reframed it through storytelling and contrast. Two dads. Two mindsets. One unforgettable lesson.

That's what you're looking for: your unique angle, not a brand-new category.

Here's a simple way to find it:

- ***Fit In:*** Identify three successful books already serving your audience. These are your neighbors on the bookshelf.

- ***Stand Out:*** Ask yourself what's missing from those books that your reader still needs.

Maybe they're too technical.
Maybe they explain *what* to do but not *how* to do it.
Maybe they overlook the emotional side of the problem.

That's your opening.

You don't have to shout louder than everyone else. You just have to say the one thing they all forgot to mention.

This is what it means to own your clarity.
It's not about inventing something new. It's about presenting something *true* in a way that's unmistakably yours.

So, what's your version of that?

What do you see, feel, or teach that everyone else misses?
What truth have you lived that your industry keeps overlooking?

What makes your way of solving the problem feel more human, practical, or doable?

That's your edge. That's your difference.

And the moment you find it, your book stops competing with others and starts complementing them.
Readers don't have to choose between your book and theirs. They'll buy both.
Because yours finishes the sentence the others started.

From Expert to Guide... Positioning for Authority

Most authors think authority comes from how much they know.
It doesn't.

It comes from how clearly they can help someone else win.

That's the shift... from *expert* to *guide.*

> *Experts talk about themselves.*
> *Guides talk about their reader's journey.*

If you've ever read a book that felt like one long résumé, you know what I mean.
You reach page twenty and think, *"Okay, I get it... you're impressive. Now can we talk about me?"*

Readers don't want a teacher lecturing from the podium.

They want a mentor walking beside them.

It's the difference between saying, *"Here's what I did,"* and *"Here's what you can do."*

Think about it like a movie.
In every great story, the hero faces a problem they can't solve alone. Then the guide shows up with the plan, the tools, and the belief that the hero can win.
Harry had Dumbledore (*Harry Potter*).
Neo had Morpheus (*The Matrix*).
Tony Stark had Nick Fury (*The Avengers*).

Your reader has you.

You're the guide who's been through the struggle and found a way out. Your job isn't to be the hero of your book. It's to make your reader the hero of their own.

John Nemo built his entire business on this principle. When he left his corporate job and started from scratch, he didn't call himself the "CEO of Nemo Media Group." That meant nothing to anyone.
Instead, his LinkedIn headline said, *"I help debt collection agencies attract new clients and increase revenue."*

That one sentence changed everything.
Within ninety days, he'd generated $135,000 in new business... not by shouting about himself, but by showing his audience he understood *them*.

That's how authority works.

It's not about big titles or fancy credentials.
It's about clarity, empathy, and credibility through results.

When readers pick up your book, they should instantly know three things:
Who it's for, what problem it solves, and what result it promises.

When readers feel seen, they trust you.
When they trust you, they buy from you.
And when they buy from you—not just once, but again and again—that's when you become the authority in your space.

So don't aim to impress. Aim to impact.
That's what real authority does.

Align Your Book With Your Business Goals

Writing a book is exciting. But here's what most authors get wrong: they treat their book like a destination when it's actually the beginning.

> *Your book isn't the finish line. It's the foundation of your business ecosystem.*
> *It's not just something you sell. It's what sells everything else.*

Every great authority book serves a larger purpose. It leads readers somewhere... into your business, your ecosystem, your world.

If you stop at "just writing a book," you'll end up with a beautiful project that inspires people... and then leaves them hanging. But when you connect your book to your business goals, it becomes a bridge... one that guides readers from inspiration to action, from *"That's interesting"* to *"I need to work with you."*

Think of your book as the front door to your business. The question is, *what do you want readers to find when they step inside?*

- If you're a coach, your book should introduce your signature method—the big picture of what you do—and invite readers to explore your programs for deeper support.

- If you're a consultant, your book should make decision-makers think, *"This person understands our challenges better than we do.*

- If you're a speaker, your book should position you as the voice audiences want to hear onstage.

This isn't about being pushy or salesy. It's about alignment.

In the *Publish, Promote, Monetize* journey, *Monetize* doesn't mean chasing royalties. It means creating ripple effects—turning one book into clients, speaking engagements, partnerships, courses, or recurring income.

That's why your Big Idea has to make strategic sense.

Every chapter, every story, and every insight should serve one purpose: helping your reader solve a problem that directly connects to what your business already does.

When your book delivers value upfront, it earns permission to lead readers to the next step. And when that next step naturally aligns with your business, monetization stops feeling like marketing; it feels like momentum.

So before you outline your chapters, take a moment to connect the dots.

Ask yourself:

What transformation do I want readers to experience by the end of my book?
How does that transformation tie directly to what I offer?
Where do I want them to go next, and how will my book point them there?

When those answers are clear, your book stops being a creative project and becomes your most powerful business asset.

It positions you not just as someone with something to say, but as someone worth following.

That's how you build a book that fuels a business, not a book that sits on a shelf.

The Transformation Statement

If you can't describe what your book *does* in one clear sentence, you don't have a Big Idea yet; you have a brainstorm.

That sentence is your *Transformation Statement.*
It's the heartbeat of your book... the before-and-after promise that tells your reader exactly what's in it for them.

Here's the formula:

My book helps [audience] go from [problem] to [result].

Simple. Focused. Magnetic.

This one line keeps you anchored while you write. It also keeps your marketing and business perfectly aligned.

Let's look at a few examples:

- *"My book helps new entrepreneurs go from guessing their next move to building a business with clarity and confidence."*

- *"My book helps coaches go from chasing clients to attracting opportunities through authority positioning."*

- *"My book helps professionals go from invisible online to recognized experts in their niche."*

See how that works? Each statement names a clear audience, a painful starting point, and a meaningful result.

It's the same logic behind every strong brand message: *clarity sells.*

And that clarity is what gives your book direction.

Without it, you'll try to write everything you know instead of the one thing your reader actually needs. You'll chase ideas, pile on chapters, and lose the reader halfway through.

When your Transformation Statement is clear, it becomes your compass.
It shapes your title.
It defines your outline.
It guides every example, story, and insight.

And here's the best part: it also becomes the bridge to your business.

If your book takes readers from problem to result, your programs, products, or services should help them go even further.

The book is step one. Your business is step two.

That's how you build a system, not just a story.

So before you write another paragraph, take a moment to fill in the blanks:

My book helps [audience] go from [problem] to [result].

Now read it out loud.

Does it sound like something people would instantly say yes to?
Does it connect directly to what your business already does?
Does it promise a transformation that's specific and valuable?

If the answer is yes, congratulations... you've nailed the core of your book.

Now you're not just writing for readers.
You're building a roadmap for clients.

The Three Paths to Publishing (and Why Most Authors Choose the Wrong One)

Once you've nailed your Big Idea, it's tempting to think the hard part is over.
You've got the message, the vision, maybe even the first few chapters.
Now all that's left is "getting published," right?

Not exactly.

Because *how* you publish is just as important as *what* you publish. And it's one of the biggest decisions that will shape your book's success... creatively, financially, and strategically.

Let's walk through the three main paths authors take and why most end up choosing the wrong one.

1. Traditional Publishing

This is the route most people still dream about—signing with a big name like *Penguin Random House* or *HarperCollins,* landing an advance, and seeing your book stacked in airport bookstores.

It sounds glamorous. And it used to be the only way to get published.

But here's the fine print. Traditional publishers are investors, not fairy godmothers. They're betting on books that can sell big, not necessarily books that can build your authority or your business.

If you land a deal, you'll likely give up creative control, rights, royalties, and launch decisions. You'll wait months, sometimes years, before your book sees daylight. And unless your name already moves copies, you'll still be doing most of the marketing yourself.

Traditional publishing can still make sense if you're already a public figure, have a large platform, or your book's purpose is mass-market visibility. But for most entrepreneurs and experts, it's the slowest, least flexible way to build momentum.

2. Self-Publishing

Then there's the opposite extreme... *do it yourself.*

With platforms like *Amazon Kindle Direct Publishing (KDP)* and *In-gramSpark,* anyone can publish a book in a matter of days.
You keep your rights, your royalties, and your creative freedom.

The upside? Speed and control.
The downside? Everything else is on you.

You're the writer, designer, editor, and marketing department all in one.
And while self-publishing gives you freedom, it also brings risk.
Without professional execution, even the best idea can look amateur.

Readers don't judge your effort; they judge your presentation.
A poorly edited or badly designed book can hurt your brand more than help it.

Self-publishing works beautifully for hands-on authors who have time to learn the process and enjoy doing everything themselves.
But if you're a business owner or expert with limited time, that freedom can quickly turn into a full-time job.

3. Hybrid Publishing

Then there's the middle path... *Hybrid Publishing.*

Hybrid combines the best of both worlds: the creative freedom and own-ership of self-publishing with the professional polish and strategy of tra-ditional publishing.

You keep control of your rights and your vision, but you don't have to figure everything out alone.

A good hybrid partner provides the editorial, design, and marketing expertise that make your book look and perform like it came from a major publisher, while keeping it aligned with your business goals.

That last part matters.

Because for entrepreneurs, coaches, and consultants, your book isn't just a creative project.

It's a positioning tool. A credibility engine. The front door to your ecosystem.

Hybrid publishing ensures your book doesn't just look great; it works for your business.

There's no single right path for everyone.

Each one has trade-offs in time, control, cost, and purpose.

But if your goal is to build authority, expand your reach, and connect your book directly to your business, the hybrid path is usually the smartest play.

The goal isn't just to publish a book.
It's to publish with purpose and strategy.

Bringing It All Together

You've just crossed the first real milestone: shifting from thinking like a writer to thinking like an authority.

You're not chasing inspiration anymore. You're building intention.

Your Big Idea isn't just a random thought anymore. It's a message that connects purpose with positioning... one that fits a real market, solves a real problem, and aligns with your business goals.

You've learned that your book isn't about you. It's about your reader... about the problem you help them solve and the result you help them achieve.

You've seen that your story isn't the headline. It's the proof.

You're not writing to share; you're writing to serve.

You've discovered how to *fit in* with what already works in your market while *standing out* with your own experience, voice, and approach.

You've redefined authority... not as "knowing more," but as *helping better*.

This is where every great author-entrepreneur begins... not with ideas, but with clarity.

Clarity about who you're helping.

Clarity about what transformation you promise.

Clarity about how your book fuels your business instead of sitting outside it.

So before you move on to the next chapter, take a few minutes to reflect.

What problem do you want to be known for solving?

If your book could create one transformation for readers, what would it be?

How does that transformation connect to your business today?

Write your answers down. Keep them where you can see them. Let them guide every decision you make from this point forward... your title, your outline, your marketing, everything.

This is where your publishing journey truly starts:

not with writing words, but with understanding your purpose.

You've nailed your Big Idea.

Now it's time to bring it to life.

Step 2: Know Your Reader Better Than They Know Themselves

Stop Writing for "Everyone"

LET'S START WITH A quick reality check: if your book is for everyone, it's actually for no one.

I get it. You've got a big heart and a message you believe could help anyone who reads it. You want to reach the masses, not a small group. But here's the problem: when you try to talk to everyone, nobody feels like you're talking to them.

You've seen those motivational posters, right? A mountain in the background and a quote like *"Dreams don't work unless you do."* It's inspiring... for about three seconds. Then you scroll past it.

That's exactly what happens when your book tries to speak to the world... it fades into background noise.

The fastest way to lose your audience is to not choose one.

Every bestselling author you admire started by choosing *someone*. Not *everyone*. Not "all humans between 18 and 99." One kind of person with one kind of problem.

Brené Brown didn't try to help the entire planet understand emotion. She spoke to people who felt small, ashamed, and disconnected—and in doing so, she reached the world.

James Clear didn't write *Atomic Habits* for productivity experts. He wrote it for people who just wanted to stop breaking promises to themselves.

And *Mark Manson*? He didn't invent not caring. He just gave burned-out millennials permission to drop the fake positivity and breathe again.

See the pattern?

They didn't shout at everyone. They whispered to someone.

That's your job as an author... to know exactly who that *"someone"* is.

> *Here's the truth: readers don't buy pages. They buy possibilities.*
> *Your book is just the bridge that helps them get there.*

Why Knowing Your Reader Changes Everything

If you've ever wondered why some books take off while others barely get a polite clap, here's the truth: clarity gets attention, but understanding creates connection.
You need both. Clarity makes your message visible. Understanding makes it personal.

Most authors start with what they want to say. The great ones start with what their readers need to hear.

Knowing your reader changes everything: your title, your tone, your stories, and even your timing. It's the difference between giving a lecture and having a conversation.

Let's be honest. Nobody wakes up thinking, *"You know what I'd love to do today? Read a 250-page monologue from a stranger."*

People read because they're searching for something: an answer, a spark, a way out.

When *Simon Sinek* wrote *Start With Why*, he tapped into something deeper than motivation. He spoke to leaders who were successful on paper but restless inside… people chasing results without meaning. He gave them language for a feeling they couldn't name.

When *Mel Robbins* created *The 5 Second Rule*, she wasn't showing off her credentials. She was speaking to people stuck under the weight of their own hesitation, desperate for one reason to move.

Or look at *Charles Duhigg*, author of *The Power of Habit*. He didn't invent behavior change; he revealed how tiny cues drive every action we take. His genius wasn't complexity; it was showing readers how their brains already work, then giving them control back.

That's what happens when you know your reader. You stop writing from your own head and start writing from theirs.

You stop asking, *"What should I say?"* and start asking, *"What are they dying to hear?"*

When your book gives people the words for feelings they couldn't explain, you earn instant trust.

You become the voice that finally says what they've been thinking all along.

That's when connection happens...
not when you talk about yourself, but when you prove you understand them.

Get Inside Their Head (and Heart)

If you really want to connect with your reader, you have to go deeper than demographics. Forget age, gender, and job titles. You're not running ads. You're writing a book.

Your reader isn't a statistic. They're a living, breathing person with fears, dreams, and a search history full of questions they'd never say out loud.

To write something that actually moves people, you need to step into their world and stay there long enough to feel what they feel.

What keeps them awake at night?
What makes them slam the steering wheel on the way to work?
What lie do they tell themselves just to get through another day?

When you can answer those questions, you'll never run out of things to say.

Look at *Brené Brown*. Her genius wasn't discovering vulnerability. It was naming what everyone else was too afraid to admit. She took private shame and turned it into public courage. That's not psychology. That's empathy with a megaphone.

Or *Mark Manson*. His books hit because he sounds like that brutally honest friend who says what everyone's thinking but no one else has the guts to say. He doesn't write *at* you. He writes *with* you.

And *Jay Shetty*? He makes ancient wisdom feel like a conversation over coffee. He knows his reader isn't hunting for enlightenment. They just want to feel a little less lost.

That's what knowing your reader really means. It's not about guessing their "pain points." It's about feeling them.

Because empathy always beats expertise.

No one cares how smart you are if they don't believe you understand what it's like to be them.

So stop trying to sound impressive. Start trying to sound real.

> *When your reader sees themselves in your words, they don't need a sales pitch. They feel seen.*
> *And when someone feels seen, they don't just read your book; they remember it.*

The Psychology of Connection

Every reader has a hidden reason they pick up a book, and it's almost never about the topic on the cover.

Nobody buys *10 Steps to Financial Freedom* because they love spreadsheets. They buy it because they're tired of feeling anxious every time they check their bank account.

Nobody grabs *How to Be More Confident* because they want to study psychology. They buy it because they're tired of watching life happen without them.

People don't buy books. They buy emotional relief.

And that's why understanding the psychology of connection matters.

At the heart of every bestselling book, you'll find four emotions at work: **fear, frustration, desire, and hope.**

Fear says, *"I don't want to lose."*
Frustration says, *"I'm stuck."*
Desire says, *"I want more."*
Hope whispers, *"Maybe this book will finally help."*

Think about Donald Miller. In *Building a StoryBrand*, he flipped the script: instead of telling companies to "sell harder," he taught them to *listen better.* His success came from turning marketing into empathy... helping readers see their customer as the hero.

And here's the payoff. That one book didn't just sell copies; it built a seven-figure business. Today, Miller runs *StoryBrand,* a full-scale agency that helps companies clarify their message and grow their revenue... all born from the framework he shared in his book. His story proves that when you truly understand your reader, your book doesn't end at the last page. It becomes the start of something much bigger.

Josh Nelson did something similar. His book *The Seven-Figure Agency Roadmap* began as a way to document his lessons running a digital-marketing agency. It resonated so strongly with other agency owners that it turned into a thriving coaching company, helping hundreds of entrepreneurs scale past seven figures.

Both stories are proof that empathy isn't just good for connection; it's good for business. When your book speaks directly to your audience's pain, it doesn't just build trust. It builds momentum that multiplies.

Jay Shetty does this too. He takes ancient ideas and translates them into stories that sound like conversations with a friend. He doesn't just teach mindfulness; he helps readers feel understood in the middle of their chaos. That empathy built an audience of millions and a global brand that started with one idea: making wisdom go viral.

Mel Robbins nailed this as well. In *The High 5 Habit*, she didn't preach self-love from a stage. She spoke to people who could cheer for everyone else but couldn't bring themselves to do the same. That honesty didn't just create a bestseller; it sparked a movement. Her frameworks turned into viral talks, sold-out events, and an online community that keeps growing because she understood the reader before she tried to teach them.

And James Clear? He didn't sell a framework. He sold relief: the peace of finally sticking to a habit that lasts. *Atomic Habits* didn't just make readers feel seen; it built a loyal following of people obsessed with small, steady improvement. That focus turned one clear message into a publishing phenomenon and a multimillion-dollar brand.

Every great author becomes fluent in their reader's emotional language.

They listen to how people describe their pain, their confusion, and their hope... then reflect it back with clarity. That's what I call *mirror language.* When your reader sees their exact thoughts written on the page, it feels like you've been sitting inside their head.

That's when connection happens.

Not because you're persuasive, but because you're *understanding.*

And once your reader feels understood, you can take them anywhere... from fear to confidence, from confusion to clarity, from frustration to freedom.

> *You don't win readers by talking at them.*
> *You win them by showing them they're not alone.*

Where to Find Your Reader in the Wild

So, how do you actually find this mysterious reader you're supposed to understand better than they understand themselves?

Easy. You stalk them.

Okay, not in the "dark hoodie and binoculars" kind of way. I mean in the digital sense... the professional kind of stalking that marketers call "research."

> *Your readers are everywhere, talking about their struggles for*
> *free on the internet.*
> *You just have to listen.*

Start with ***Amazon*** **reviews**. But skip the five-star love letters. The real gold lives in the one- and two-star reviews. That's where readers stop being polite and start being honest.

When someone writes, *"This book had good ideas, but it didn't tell me how to actually apply them,"* what they're really saying is, *"I'm tired of vague advice. I need something practical."*

When another person says, *"I felt like the author didn't get my situation,"* they're telling you exactly what to fix. That's a flashing neon sign saying, "Connect before you teach."

Next, hang out in *Facebook* groups and *LinkedIn* threads where your target audience spends time. People overshare there like it's an Olympic sport.

Look for the posts that start with *"Does anyone else struggle with..."* Those are treasure maps. Every comment, every complaint, every *"ugh, this is* me," is a window into what your reader feels.

If you want the unfiltered truth, visit *Reddit*. It's where people drop their filters completely. You'll find everything from exhausted parents venting about burnout to entrepreneurs confessing they're scared they picked the wrong path.

Want to go deeper? Listen to podcasts your audience follows. Read the episode reviews. People will tell you exactly what they loved and what bored them.

Every platform is full of clues about what your readers want, what they're sick of, and what they can't find anywhere else.

Your job isn't to copy other authors. It's to decode the conversations your readers are already having.

> *When you start listening like that, you stop guessing what to write about and start writing what they already care about.*

And that's when your message stops feeling like marketing and starts feeling like connection.

Your Reader Avatar... The One-Person Rule

Now that you've found your readers out in the wild, it's time to bring one of them to life.

No, not in a Frankenstein way. More like in a "finally, I know who I'm talking to" way.

> *Your Reader Avatar is that one person your book is written for. Not a crowd. Not a demographic. One real human being who represents your ideal reader.*

And please, let's skip the cheesy marketing exercises. You don't need "Entrepreneur Emily, 37, drives a Tesla, drinks oat milk, and loves hiking." That's not a person; that's a smoothie with Wi-Fi.

What you need is a mental picture of a real life, with real struggles.

If you can't imagine what your reader eats for breakfast, you don't know them well enough.

What does their day actually look like?
When do they feel most defeated?
What do they tell their friends they're "fine" about when they're really not?

Your job is to understand their world so deeply that your book feels like it was written inside it.

Think of *Mel Robbins*. She doesn't write to "everyone who procrastinates." She writes to the version of herself who used to hit snooze on her life. That's why her work hits so hard... she's not guessing what her readers feel; she *remembers*.

Or *Simon Sinek*. He's not talking to every employee with a paycheck. He's talking to the visionary leader buried inside you: the one who wants work to matter again.

That's how you find your voice.

Try this: picture yourself across from your ideal reader at a coffee shop. They take a deep breath and say, *"Can I be honest with you? Here's what I'm really struggling with..."*

Now write what they'd say next. Don't overthink it. That's your gold.

And here's something most authors miss: your niche isn't random; it's you, a few chapters ago... your previous version of yourself.

The person you used to be before you figured things out? That's your reader. You already know their fears, frustrations, and blind spots because you've lived them.

That's why your story matters. Not as a spotlight, but as a mirror. You're not writing from a pedestal; you're reaching back to your earlier self and saying, *"Hey, I found a way through this. Let me show you."*

When you see your niche as your previous version, empathy becomes effortless. You don't have to imagine what they feel. You remember.

When that person becomes clear in your mind, writing stops feeling like a guessing game. You know what to say, how to say it, and why it matters.

> *When you write for one, your words sound like a friend's advice.*
> *When you write for everyone, you sound like an ad.*
> *And no one curls up with an ad.*

Speak Their Language

Once you know who your reader is, your next job is to speak their language. Not *down* to them. Not *at* them. *With* them.

Because words build trust... and the quickest way to lose it is to sound like you're auditioning for a corporate memo.

If your reader says, *"I feel stuck,"* don't write, *"You may be experiencing a period of stagnation."* That's not empathy. That's anesthesia.

Your job isn't to sound smart. It's to sound familiar.

That's why *Gary Vee* doesn't say, *"Execute a consistent content strategy."* He says, *"Post it. Test it. Learn from it."* Short. Sharp. Human.

Donald Miller gets it too. In *Building a StoryBrand*, he doesn't hide behind buzzwords or theory. He talks like a friend explaining something over lunch. That's why his readers don't just understand; they act.

And *Rachel Hollis*? She doesn't sound like a life coach reading off a script. She sounds like your best friend who's finally telling you the truth. That's why her words hit... they're simple, honest, and full of heart.

If your audience uses emojis, talk like someone who gets what "" means. If they spend their mornings on podcasts, write like someone who listens too.

You're not trying to impress your reader. You're trying to connect with them.

Connection doesn't happen through fancy words. It happens through shared ones.

So drop the jargon. Ditch the "therefores." Stop writing like you're in a boardroom.

Write like you're in their inbox.

The moment your words sound like theirs, they stop feeling like readers and start feeling like you wrote the book just for them.

Bring It Home

Let's bring it all together.

You can't write a book that connects until you know who you're writing for. Not a crowd. Not a category. A person.

When you understand your reader's world—their fears, frustrations, and secret hopes—your book stops sounding like advice and starts feeling like relief.

That's what great authors do. They don't write at people. They write *for* them.

So before you move on, take a few minutes to think about your reader: that one person you've been picturing through this chapter.

Grab a notebook and jot down a few notes while it's fresh:

- *Who's the one person your book is really for?*

- *What keeps them up at night?*

- *What problem are they done trying to solve alone?*

- *If they picked up your book, what line would make them smile and say, "Finally, someone gets it"?*

Don't overthink it; just write what feels real.

The clearer you see them, the easier every word of your book will come.

Remember, you don't need a bigger audience. You need a deeper one.

When you know your reader that well, your book doesn't just speak to them; it sticks with them long after the last page.

Step 3: Reverse-Engineer Success

The Myth of the Original Idea

EVERY NEW AUTHOR WANTS to be a genius.

You can picture them: latte in hand, staring at a blinking cursor, whispering, *"I just need an idea no one's ever written before."*

Yeah... good luck with that.

> *Here's the truth: originality is overrated.*
> *The authors who win aren't inventing new ideas; they're refreshing proven ones.*

You don't have to create something no one's seen. You just have to say something everyone already feels... but in a way they've never quite heard before.

James Clear didn't invent habits. He organized them.
Mark Manson didn't invent not caring. He made it hilarious.
Brené Brown didn't invent vulnerability. She made it universal.

These authors didn't start from zero. They started from *research*. They studied what readers were already devouring and asked, *"How can I make this simpler, faster, or more real?"*

So if you've ever said, *"No one's ever written a book like mine,"* ... be careful: that might mean no one's looking for it.

Readers don't crave something completely new; they want the familiar done better.

Originality is about perspective, not invention.
Don't aim to be first; aim to be the one who finally makes it stick.

Steal Like an Author

Let's clear something up: every successful author is a thief.
Not a plagiarist, but a pattern pirate. They borrow what works, remix it with their own story, and sell it back with flavor.

Picasso said, *"Good artists copy. Great artists steal."*
Writers just do it with more caffeine.

Tim Ferriss did it with *The 4-Hour Workweek*. He didn't invent "lifestyle design." He took ideas from productivity, psychology, and travel hacking... then packaged them for exhausted professionals dreaming of escape.

Mel Robbins didn't invent motivation. She made it practical and human. One rule. Five seconds. A global brand.

Donald Miller didn't invent storytelling. He just taught entrepreneurs how to finally use it to sell something.

None of that is theft; it's pattern recognition.

The pros don't guess their way to success; they study what's already working and ask, *"Why does this connect?"*

It's like music. Every hit shares a few chords, but the magic is in the remix: the rhythm, the delivery, and the energy that make it feel new.

So yes, go ahead... steal like an author.

Scroll through Amazon like a detective, not a dreamer:

- *What promises are bestselling books making?*

- *How are they framing transformation?*

- *What tone are they using: friendly coach, bold challenger, or quiet guide?*

- *Where do readers light up... and where do they lose interest?*

That's your research lab.

Because the goal isn't to copy. It's to decode the DNA of success and then rewrite it in your voice.

> *In publishing, originality doesn't start with invention. It starts with investigation.*

Deconstruct the Bestseller Blueprint

Every bestselling book follows a pattern. Once you see it, you can't unsee it.

Let's pull it apart, piece by piece.

1. Title and Subtitle: The Promise, the Outcome, the Hook

Your title is your billboard. It has one job: to stop people mid-scroll and make them think, *"This is exactly what I need."*

Look at the pros:

- *Atomic Habits:* clear and memorable, built on a metaphor everyone gets.

- *Deep Work:* crisp and disciplined, promising productivity through focus.

- *The Subtle Art of Not Giving a F**:* bold, funny, and impossible to ignore.

- *The 5 Second Rule:* simple, relatable, instantly usable.

Each of these books promises a transformation in plain English. No riddles. No overthinking.

Short titles grab attention, and a sharp subtitle closes the sale.

2. Covers That Belong and Get Clicked

Your cover isn't art. It's marketing.

On Amazon, readers don't browse; they blink.
You've got a second to make them stop scrolling.

Great covers send a clear signal: *This book is for you.*

Use clean fonts, smart colors, and minimal clutter.

When *Atomic Habits* came out, its clean gold and white design screamed "clarity."
When Gary Vee released *Jab, Jab, Jab, Right Hook,* it looked alive: bold, loud, and full of energy.

Design to belong, not to brag. If your cover doesn't look like it fits your genre, readers will assume it doesn't fit them either.

3. Categories and Keywords: The Small Pond Strategy

Amazon isn't just a bookstore. It's a search engine in disguise.

Most authors throw their book into giant categories like "Business" or "Self-Help" and hope for the best. That's like whispering at a concert.

Smart authors go smaller. They find categories where demand is strong but competition is low.

You don't need a million readers. You need the right ten thousand. That's how bestsellers are born... one niche at a time.

4. Review Mining: Listen Before You Write

Want to know what readers really want? Read their complaints.

One-star reviews are free consulting sessions from your audience.
They'll tell you exactly what's missing:
"Too vague."
"All theory, no examples."
"Loved the topic but couldn't finish it."

Perfect. That's your opening. Write the book that fixes it.

Then read the five-star reviews. Those show you what readers love. You'll start to see patterns: clarity, honesty, and stories that feel real.

That's not guessing. That's research.

5. Chapter Flow: Promise, Story, Action

Every great book moves the reader forward, not just through pages but through change.

Each chapter starts with a promise, delivers it through a story or example, and ends with something the reader can do or reflect on.

That's the rhythm behind *The 5 Second Rule, Atomic Habits,* and *Start With Why.*
Each chapter gives you one idea that sticks, one story that proves it, and one action that makes it real.

Readers don't just finish those books; they live them.

When you understand this blueprint, writing stops feeling like guesswork and starts feeling like strategy.

Smart Authors Use AI Wisely

AI is like coffee for your research process... it can make everything faster, but drink too much and you'll start making weird decisions.

Used right, it's a fantastic assistant. You can use AI to research categories, study bestselling titles, summarize reader reviews, or organize keyword lists in minutes. What used to take hours of scrolling and caffeine now happens before your mug gets cold.

But here's the deal: AI can't replace you.

It doesn't know your stories, your setbacks, or what it felt like to stare at your first draft and wonder if anyone would care. It can mimic language, but it can't mimic life.

AI is great for research, structure, and clarity checks—but not for emotion, nuance, or heart. It can predict patterns, not passion.

And a quick heads-up: platforms like *Amazon* and *IngramSpark* now ask authors to disclose if AI was used. Nobody knows yet how they'll treat AI-heavy books in the long run, but one thing's certain—authenticity will always win.

So use AI as your assistant, not your author.

Let it help you organize ideas, but don't let it tell your story.
Let it crunch data, not shape your voice.

Because no algorithm can fake what makes your book human: your scars, your hard-won lessons, and the hope that lives between your lines.

That's what readers come for. Not machine perfection; human truth.

Spot the Market Gaps

Now comes the fun part: finding what's missing.

Read enough bestsellers in your niche and you'll start hearing the same playlist on repeat: familiar ideas, similar tone, and predictable rhythm.

That's your opening.

Simon Sinek made leadership emotional again.
Mel Robbins made mindset something you could actually use.
Gary Vee made entrepreneurship louder, bolder, and more human.

None of them invented new topics. They just saw what everyone else was doing... and did it differently.

The best authors don't create demand. They serve it better.

Want proof? Go read Amazon reviews in your niche. But skip the glowing five-stars. The gold is in the complaints.

Look for comments like:

"Loved the concept, but it never got practical."
"Too much theory."
"I wanted examples I could relate to."

That's your audience handing you a checklist of opportunities.

You don't need to find a brand-new idea. You just need to deliver an existing one with more empathy, clarity, or courage.

Readers aren't looking for something they've never heard of. They're looking for something that finally *works*.

> *Forget chasing brand-new ideas.*
> *Focus on perfecting the ones no one's executed well yet.*

Build Your Positioning Map

Once you've studied the landscape, it's time to draw your map.

Grab a blank page and list the three top books in your niche.
Then note three things about each one:

- *What they do well*

- *What they miss*

- *Who they speak to*

That last column is where your opportunity lives.

Ask yourself: *Where do I fit in this story?*

That's your Positioning Map.

Simon Sinek speaks to mission-driven leaders.
Gary Vee speaks to hustlers.
Mel Robbins speaks to overthinkers.
Tony Robbins speaks to achievers.
Brian Tracy speaks to disciplined professionals.

Who do you speak to?

Once you know that, everything else becomes easier... your title, your tone, even the color of your cover.

You're no longer guessing who your reader is. You're designing for them.

That's how you stand out on the shelf... not by shouting louder, but by showing up clearer.
In publishing, clarity beats cleverness every time.

Find the Pattern, Then Personalize It

Now comes the part that makes your book yours.

Patterns show you what works; personality makes readers remember.

Mel Robbins could've written another dry productivity book. Instead, she told a story about hitting snooze on her alarm... and millions of readers saw themselves in that moment.

Gary Vee didn't tone it down to sound professional. He wrote the way he talks... fast, raw, and honest. His audience loved it because it sounded like him.

Simon Sinek turned a simple presentation into a global movement.
Tony Robbins turned psychology into theater.
Brian Tracy turned discipline into a brand.

They all used proven structures, but made them personal.

You don't win by copying style. You win by blending structure with self.

Be strategic enough to use what works.
Be human enough to make it sound like you.

That combination—clarity, courage, and personality—is what transforms a good book into a great one.

You don't need the perfect formula.
You just need a formula that fits you.

Bring It Home

Let's end with a little tough love.

Most authors are like New Year's gym members... fired up on day one, lost by week two.

They hop on every machine for five minutes and wonder why they don't have abs by February.

That's what happens when you skip the fundamentals.

They don't study what works. They just write, upload, and pray Jeff Bezos gives them a miracle.

But not you. You're doing this differently.

You now know how the pros do it... the ones whose books built movements and multimillion-dollar brands.

Simon Sinek didn't wake up one morning and decide to *"disrupt leadership."* He studied how great leaders communicate, found the pattern, and turned it into a global mantra: *Start With Why*.

Gary Vee didn't invent hustle. He packaged it. *Crush It!* wasn't just a title; it was a caffeinated permission slip for every entrepreneur who talks with their hands.

Tony Robbins took old-school self-help principles and turned them into live theater.

Mel Robbins took one morning habit and built a global business around it.

Brian Tracy took goal-setting research and turned it into a single unforgettable image: *Eat That Frog*.

None of them guessed.

They reverse-engineered success.

They studied what was selling, what readers loved, and where the gaps were... then built books that fit in and stood out.

So before you write another word, ask yourself:

- *Which books dominate my niche right now?*

- *What patterns do they share?*

- *Where are readers still frustrated or unfulfilled?*

- *How can my story, my voice, or my system make it clearer, faster, or more human?*

Answer those questions, and you'll stop guessing what works.
You'll start designing what does.

Writing a bestseller isn't about luck. It's about understanding how the game works and learning to play it smarter.

Step 4: Craft a Book That Sells Itself

Think Like an Experience Designer, Not a Writer

IF THIS WERE AN English competition, I'd fail.
I don't write perfect sentences. I write sentences that *work*.

And that's the whole point.

Too many first-time authors get stuck trying to be "writers." They chase poetic flow, hunt down big words, and polish each paragraph like it's going to hang in a museum. Meanwhile, their readers just want to *get to the good part*.

Being a "writer" means you're focused on yourself... the craft, the structure, the style.
Being an *author* means you're focused on the *reader*... their journey, their emotions, and their transformation.

Readers don't frame your book like art; they experience it like a *Netflix* series they can't stop watching. They're not admiring your metaphors; they're measuring how useful, fun, and fast it feels.

So this isn't just about *writing for your reader*—you already know that. This is about *designing for their attention span*. You're not polishing prose;

you're engineering momentum.

Your job isn't to create pretty pages. It's to design a journey that keeps readers turning them.
You're not writing to show off your vocabulary; you're building a path that makes your reader feel progress—emotionally and mentally—with every chapter.

Think of it like this:

- A *writer* polishes. An *author* engineers.

- A *writer* obsesses over the sentence. An *author* obsesses over the *feeling* that sentence creates.

James Clear didn't become a bestseller because of his adjectives. He did it because every paragraph delivers a dopamine hit... a mini win that makes readers think, *"I can do this."*

Mel Robbins doesn't worry about semicolons; she writes like she's texting you life advice at 6 a.m.

Donald Miller doesn't craft literary poetry; he crafts clarity that sells.

So give yourself permission to stop chasing perfect prose.
Nobody's grading you. (If they are, they're probably not buying your book.)

Your real test isn't grammar. It's engagement.
If your reader can't stop reading, you've already aced it.

Structure That Keeps Readers Hooked

Every author dreams of writing a "can't put it down" book.
You know… the kind people start reading "just for ten minutes," and suddenly it's 2 a.m., and they're whispering, *"Okay, one more chapter."*

That's not luck. That's structure.

A book that sells itself is designed like a conversation that never runs out of momentum. Each chapter gives just enough satisfaction to make the reader feel progress and just enough curiosity to keep them turning the page.

Think of your book like a binge-worthy *Netflix* series.
Every episode—sorry, every chapter—needs three things:

- a ***promise***,

- a ***payoff***, and

- a ***pull*** into the next one.

Let's break that down.

1. The Promise: Why should I care?

Every chapter should open with a promise that answers the reader's silent question: *"Why should I keep reading?"*

Make it clear what problem this chapter solves or what insight they'll walk away with.

Example: *"By the end of this chapter, you'll know exactly how to stop your habits from sabotaging your goals."*

James Clear does this beautifully. Every chapter of *Atomic Habits* starts with a small, irresistible question...
"Why do habits stick?"
"How do you make a bad one disappear?"
You don't even realize you've agreed to stay until it's over.

2. The Payoff: Prove it.

Give the reader a small win: something they can nod at and think, *"That makes sense."*

That's the heartbeat of engagement. Each chapter should deliver at least one "aha" moment or useful takeaway.

Mel Robbins does this with stories. She doesn't say, *"Confidence matters."* She shows you a mom who used the *5-Second Rule* to rebuild her courage after a job loss.

Readers don't want theory. They want results... even tiny ones.

3. The Pull: What's next?

End every chapter with a spark of momentum. A question, a cliffhanger, a teaser.
Something that makes readers think, *"Well now I have to know what happens next."*

Netflix calls this a hook. Authors call it a smart strategy.

Here's a simple rhythm to steal... I call it the *Reader Loop*:

Promise → Story → Lesson → Action → Next Step.

If you keep that rhythm consistent, readers start trusting you.
They know every chapter will reward them. They relax, they engage, and—most importantly—they finish.

And if I'm doing my job right, that's exactly what's happening in this book right now.
Each "Step" gives you a promise, a payoff, and a pull into the next one.
(At least, that's what I *hope* is happening. Otherwise, this would be awkward.)

That's the secret most authors miss.
Amazon doesn't reward books for *being read once.*
It rewards books that *get finished,* reviewed, and recommended.
The more readers stay with you, the more the algorithm stays with you too.

So don't think of structure as a "writing trick." It's your reader-retention system.
When you design your chapters for momentum, you're not just helping readers; you're training *Amazon* to love your book.

Clarity That Converts

If writing were a spelling bee, I'd have been eliminated in round one.

But luckily, readers don't care about perfect English. They care about whether you make sense... fast.

Here's the truth: clarity sells. Clever confuses.

A lot of authors try to sound "smart." They use big words, long sentences, and metaphors that require a decoder ring. It might impress your old English teacher, but it'll exhaust your readers.

When readers have to stop and reread your sentence, you've already lost them.
If they have to *Google* your word choice, they'll never finish your book... and if they never finish, *Amazon* will never show it to anyone else.

Think about the authors dominating your feed: James Clear, Mel Robbins, Gary Vee, Brené Brown, and Mark Manson.
None of them write like English professors. They write like humans who figured something out and want to share it before their coffee gets cold.

Clarity doesn't mean "dumb it down." It means "make it stick."
It means saying the one thing your reader really needs to hear... in the simplest, most honest way possible.

James Clear says, *"You don't rise to the level of your goals; you fall to the level of your systems."*
One line. Boom. That sentence sold more books than most authors write in a lifetime.

Rachel Hollis could easily sound like a life coach reading off a script, but she doesn't. She talks like your honest best friend, which is why readers lean in.

And Mark Schultz, in *Make Peace with the Mirror,* proves that plain talk can still be powerful... you don't need big words when you've got big truth.

Here's a funny thing *Amazon* doesn't advertise: the more readers highlight and share your sentences, the more visible your book becomes.
That means every underlined sentence is free marketing.

So your goal isn't to sound brilliant. It's to be *quotable.*
If readers can copy-paste your line into a tweet or highlight it on *Kindle,* they're doing your promotion for you.

Clarity multiplies connection. Cleverness creates confusion.
If your reader has to slow down, they'll stop. If they can quote you, they'll spread you.

Before you move on, try this quick gut check:
Would I actually say this out loud?
If not, simplify it until it sounds like something you'd text a friend... not present at a board meeting.

Because if readers understand you faster, they'll trust you sooner. And when they trust you, they buy... not just your book, but everything that comes after it.

Design for Engagement (Layout, Flow, and Readability)

Here's a secret nobody tells you: readers don't "read" your book; they *scan* it.
Especially online. Especially on *Kindle.*
If your pages look like an academic essay, their eyes will bounce faster than

a bad *YouTube* ad.

Readers don't think in paragraphs; they think in rhythm.
That's why your book should *look* like it's easy to read... short paragraphs, generous spacing, and clean subheadings.

Think of your layout like a breathing exercise.
Each paragraph is an inhale. Each line break is an exhale.
If you make your readers hold their breath too long, they'll pass out... or worse, quit reading.

And here's the kicker: layout isn't just for aesthetics. It directly impacts engagement.
Amazon's algorithm tracks reading behavior.
When people highlight, scroll smoothly, and finish chapters, it's a signal that your book is enjoyable, and that makes Amazon recommend it more often.

Translation?
Good formatting isn't about design. It's about *discovery*.

If you've ever opened a book and thought, *"Whoa, this feels heavy,"* you've already lost trust before reading a single word.
Clean design says, *"Relax, this will be easy."*
And when readers relax, they stay.

Here are a few quick layout rules of thumb:

1. **Break up your text.**
   Keep paragraphs short... three to five lines max. Anything longer feels like homework.

2. **Use subheadings generously.**

   They're not just dividers; they're invitations. Every subheading says, *"Hey, something valuable's coming up."*

3. **Vary sentence rhythm.**

   Mix short, punchy lines with slightly longer ones. That's what keeps the voice alive.

4. **Make it scannable and stress-free.**

   Break information into bite-size chunks and highlight only what truly matters. The easier your book feels on the eyes, the longer readers stick with you... and that's what counts.

5. **Give visual breathing room.**

   White space is your friend. Think of it as silence between your best jokes... it gives your ideas space to land.

When readers feel comfortable on the page, they'll trust you with their attention.

And attention, not language, is the currency of every bestseller.

Your words can be brilliant, but if your layout screams "textbook," nobody will stick around long enough to see it.

So treat your book's design like your reader's comfort zone.

Because if your book *feels* easy to read, people won't just finish it; they'll tell others, *"It's such a quick, enjoyable read."*

And that sentence, right there, is the best review you could ever ask for.

Build the Transformation Path

Now that your book *looks* good and reads smoothly, let's make sure it *does* something.

Readers don't pick up books because they're bored. They pick them up because they want to change something... their habits, their mindset, their results, or sometimes just how they see themselves.

Your job is to take them somewhere.

Think of your book like a GPS. Every chapter should start with "*You are here*" and end with "*Here's how to get there.*"

The magic is in the *movement*. Readers need to feel like they're progressing. That's what transformation really is... small, consistent wins that add up to a big "aha."

The best books don't drown readers in information. They deliver *progress*.

James Clear doesn't teach the science of habits; he helps you become the kind of person who follows through.
Mel Robbins doesn't explain motivation; she helps you move before your brain talks you out of it.
Jay Shetty doesn't give you wisdom quotes; he translates them into small, modern actions that feel doable right now.

Each of them turns insight into motion... not just knowledge but momentum.

Here's a simple rule to follow:

If a reader can finish a chapter and *do* something differently—even a tiny action, a shift in perspective, or a better question—you've won.

That's what separates "good" from "impactful."

To help you design that transformation path, use the **Before/After** model:

- **Before:** Where is my reader right now?
  Confused, stuck, overwhelmed, curious?

- **After:** What will they believe, know, or do differently by the end of this chapter?

If you can define that clearly, every section you write will have purpose.

It also keeps you from padding chapters with fluff.
If a paragraph doesn't move the reader toward the "after," it doesn't belong there.

Think of it like building a staircase.
Every chapter is one step up.
Readers shouldn't have to leap or guess what's next; they should feel gently guided.

By the final page, they should feel two things:

- *"I've changed."*

- *"I know what to do next."*

That's transformation. That's why they'll leave a review. That's why they'll share your book.

When your book helps someone move forward, they talk about it... and that talk drives discovery. Every finished chapter, every shared highlight, every "you've got to read this" moment tells Amazon your book matters. That's how meaning turns into momentum.

Reader Experience Leads to Algorithm Love

Here's the twist most authors miss: *Amazon* doesn't judge your writing; it tracks your readers. It measures what they do—not what you say—and that data decides how visible your book becomes.

If readers buy your book and stop halfway through, *Amazon* takes note... and they do track this on *Kindle*.
If they finish it, highlight passages, and leave a review, *Amazon* takes note of that too.
Guess which one gets recommended more?

That means the quality of the reading experience literally affects your visibility.
The more readers engage, the more Amazon's algorithm says, "People like this... let's show it to more people."

So yes, structure, clarity, and design aren't just good writing habits. They're discoverability strategies in disguise.

Think about it like this:

- A strong opening keeps readers from bouncing.

- A clean layout keeps them scrolling.

- Chapter payoffs make them feel progress.

- Transformational moments earn emotional investment.

All of that signals to *Amazon* that your book is *working*.

This is where art quietly turns into analytics.
When your book feels good to read, it performs better... not just with humans, but with algorithms.

That's why some authors with modest followings end up outselling big names.
They don't buy their way into visibility; they *design* for it.

Readers stay longer, finish stronger, and tell the algorithm, "*This book is worth recommending.*"
That's the compounding effect of experience.

Your book isn't just a message. It's data.
Every highlight, review, and completed chapter is a signal that feeds the system.
So before you think about keywords or categories (that's Step 5), make sure the book itself earns attention first.

> *A book that keeps readers turning the pages doesn't just sell itself; it convinces Amazon to sell it for you.*

Quick Gut Check

Before you move on, take a quick breath... and a quick reality check.

You've just built the foundation of a book that not only connects with readers but also keeps them hooked long enough for *Amazon* to notice.

This isn't about writing pretty sentences anymore; it's about creating an experience that earns attention, trust, and love.

Ask yourself three simple questions:

1. *Would a stranger—not your best friend or editor—actually keep reading past page ten?*

2. *Does every chapter deliver progress, not padding?*

3. *Would I quote myself if I found this line on a Kindle highlight?*

If you can answer *"yes"* to all three, you're ready.

You've crafted a book that isn't just read; it's remembered.

Next comes discoverability... turning all that effort into visibility.

You've built a book worth reading; now let's make sure the right readers can actually see it.

So grab that coffee and turn the page... it's time to learn how to make *Amazon* fall in love with your book too.

Step 5: Optimize for the Amazon Search Engine

Amazon Isn't Just a Bookstore; It's a Search Engine with a Credit Card

HERE'S SOMETHING MOST FIRST-TIME authors miss: more than half of all book sales now begin with a search on *Amazon*.

That means readers aren't wandering digital aisles; they're typing with *intent to buy*.

And that changes everything.

> *Amazon isn't just a bookstore; it's the world's largest search-and-purchase engine... where discovery and checkout happen in the same breath.*

When you understand that, you stop writing for browsers and start positioning for buyers.

When people go to *Google*, they're curious. They're looking for information.
When they go to *Amazon*, they're looking to buy.

They don't browse for fun; they search with intent:
"How to write a business plan."
"Leadership for introverts."
"How to stop procrastinating."

And the books that appear on the first page of those searches?
Those are the ones that get bought.

Here's the uncomfortable truth: if your book isn't optimized for search, it's invisible. You can have the smartest insights, the most heartfelt message, and a cover worthy of an award... but if readers can't *find* it, none of it matters.

Amazon's algorithm (think of it as *Google's* highly caffeinated cousin) decides who wins the visibility game. It tracks clicks, conversions, and engagement... then rewards the listings that perform. The better your book converts, the more *Amazon* promotes it.

And that's the game: when you help Amazon sell, it helps you sell.

Think of *Amazon* as a data-driven librarian that knows every reader's secret wishlist.
Its job? To connect the right reader with the right book... instantly.

Once you see *Amazon* through that lens, publishing strategy changes.
You stop thinking like an author and start thinking like an architect... designing your book to be discoverable, clickable, and buyable.

Because success on *Amazon* isn't about shelf space anymore.
It's about *search space.*

So before you print those business cards that say *"Published Author,"* ask yourself:

If a stranger typed their biggest problem into Amazon right now, would my book show up?

If not... time to fix that.

Before readers even see your cover, Amazon's algorithm quietly scans the signals behind your listing—your keywords, categories, and metadata—to decide whether your book even deserves to appear. Optimization isn't decoration; it's discoverability.

Keywords: The Secret to Being Found

Let's be honest: most authors treat keywords like secret ingredients in Grandma's spaghetti sauce.
They know they're important but have no clue what's actually in them.

Here's the truth: keywords aren't magic.
They're just the exact words your readers type into *Amazon* when they're looking for help, answers, or inspiration.

And once you understand how and why people search, *Amazon* starts working for you... not against you.

Because not every search means the same thing.

There are three types of readers wandering the *Amazon* jungle:

1. ***The Researcher:*** They're in *informational mode.* Typing things like *"how to publish a book"* or *"how to grow my coaching business."* They're curious but cautious.

2. ***The Explorer:*** They're in *navigational mode.* They already know who or what they're looking for… *"James Clear," "Atomic Habits," "Tony Robbins."* They're halfway sold.

3. ***The Buyer:*** These are the gold. They're in *commercial mode.* Typing *"best book on book marketing"* or *"top nonfiction publishing guide."* They're ready to buy… they just need to find you.

If you understand these three search intents, you stop guessing. You start building your book's metadata like a mind reader.

Because every part of your listing—title, subtitle, description, backend keywords, even your *A+ Content*—is a chance to match what readers are already typing.

Let's break it down:

- ***Title:*** Clarity wins. The best titles tell readers exactly what they'll get. Think *Deep Work, The Mountain Is You,* or *Dare to Lead.* Short. Emotional. Search-friendly.

- ***Subtitle:*** This is your keyword gold mine… where you expand the promise using phrases people actually search for. Like *"Rules for Focused Success in a Distracted World"* or *"Transforming Self-Sabotage into Self-Mastery."* Simple, human, and full of real language, not jargon.

- ***Description:*** This is where you humanize the search terms. Don't stuff them. Weave them naturally into the story. Something *like "How to finally get your ideas out of your head and into a book readers love."*

- ***A+ Content:*** Those short headlines and visuals? Use them strategically. *Amazon* reads this text too... and the right phrasing can quietly boost visibility.

- ***Backend Keywords:*** You get seven KDP keyword boxes... use every one. Add long-tail phrases readers actually type, like *"how to publish a book that sells"* or *"marketing strategies for coaches."* One phrase per box. No commas. No keyword soup.

> **Pro Tip:**
>
> *Amazon* doesn't just scan your title and subtitle; it also crawls your Table of Contents and the first 20 pages of your *Look Inside* preview. That means your most important keywords should also appear naturally in your TOC and early chapters.
>
> You're not stuffing; you're reinforcing.
>
> You're teaching the algorithm what your book is about, just like you're teaching your reader.

Here's where most authors stop.

But the smart ones see *Amazon* for what it really is... not just a store, but a *testing ground*.

When you find keywords that convert—the ones readers search, click, and buy from—you're not just winning on *Amazon*.
You're discovering the language of your market.

That's the gold.

Because once you know what works here, you can take that same data and *expand your reach...* distributing through *IngramSpark* and every other major retailer with a proven keyword strategy.

In other words, *Amazon* gives you a laboratory.
You test your message.
You refine your positioning.
And when you've found the winning formula, you scale it globally.

See the pattern?
You're not tricking algorithms; you're aligning with your readers.

If someone types *"how to write a book that builds authority,"* and your title, subtitle, and metadata all whisper back, *"I can help you do exactly that,"...* you win.

> *And here's the beauty of it: Amazon literally tells you what people want.*
> *Just start typing in the search bar and watch what auto-completes.*
> *That's live data from real humans spending real money.*

You don't need a PhD in SEO.

You just need curiosity.

Think of keyword research as eavesdropping… ethically.
You're listening to what your readers are already asking for.

Because when your metadata matches their intent, *Amazon* starts doing your marketing for you.

And once you've tested and tuned your message here, you've built something far more powerful than visibility… you've built proof.

Proof you can take to every other retailer in the world.

If it sells on Amazon, it can sell anywhere.

Pro Tip:
Smart authors don't stop at *Amazon*.
They take the same high-performing keywords and use them everywhere: in their landing pages, website copy, email campaigns, and even social media captions.
Why? Because the language that drives clicks on *Amazon* is the same language that captures attention everywhere else.
You're not just optimizing for a platform; you're synchronizing your entire message around what your audience actually searches, says, and buys.

Categories: Where You Compete (and Win)

Most authors treat categories like the side salad that comes with your steak… they poke at it, ignore it, and then wonder why they're still hungry for sales.

But here's the truth: your categories decide whether your book is front and center on *Amazon*… or buried behind *Atomic Habits* and a 2012 crochet manual for retired engineers.

When you publish your book, *Amazon* lets you choose *three categories*. That's it.
And those three choices can make or break your visibility.

Once upon a time, you could email *Amazon Author Support* and politely ask to be added to up to ten categories. Technically, you still can… but let's just say the enthusiasm on the other side of that inbox has cooled. You can try it (and you should), but don't have high hopes.

Think of it as a long shot that sometimes pays off… like finding Wi-Fi on a plane.

So for now, focus on the three you *can* control.

Here's the strategy:

1. ***One big category*** where readers actually browse: something broad enough to give your book visibility.
   Example: *Business & Money > Entrepreneurship*

2. ***One medium category*** where you can hold your own.

Example: *Business & Money > Women & Business*

3. **One small, laser-targeted niche** where you can actually dominate.
   Example: *Business & Money > Time Management > Time Management for Small Business*

That mix gives you reach, credibility, and a realistic shot at that little orange "#1 Best Seller" tag... without needing to sell thousands of copies overnight.

And whatever you do, please don't just dump your book into *General Business*.
That's the category equivalent of shouting your name in a football stadium.

Here's what most authors miss: *Amazon* doesn't reward fame. It rewards relevance.
When your category precisely matches what readers are searching for, *Amazon* says, *"Ah, this book clearly belongs here... let's show it to more people."*

That's how you climb the charts.

But choose wrong, and things get weird.
I once saw a productivity book sitting in *Crafts, Hobbies & Home > Coloring Books for Grown-Ups.*
Somewhere out there, a poor shopper looking for unicorns ended up learning about morning routines.

So before you hit publish, do a little detective work.

Look up books that are performing well in your niche. Check their *Best Seller Rank* and see which categories they live in.

The top earners aren't fighting in *Business & Money*. They're hiding in micro-niches like:

- *Health, Fitness & Dieting > Stress Management > Work-Related Stress*

- *Self-Help > Communication & Social Skills > Public Speaking & Speech Writing*

- *Business & Money > Marketing & Sales > Digital Marketing*

- *Business & Money > Leadership & Motivation > Women & Business*

Those small ponds are where big fish are made.

You don't need to outsell the world… just the few authors swimming next to you.

> *So build your category mix like a strategist:*
> **One big. One medium. One you can own.**

And if you're feeling bold, go ahead and email *Amazon* to request a few more.

Maybe you'll get lucky.

Just… don't wait by your inbox.

Covers That Convert

Here's the deal: people absolutely judge a book by its cover.
Especially on *Amazon,* where your book appears as a tiny *rectangular thumbnail* fighting for attention among thousands of others.

When readers scroll, they don't see your brilliant insights, your research, or your story.
They see one image, one title, and have a split second to decide if you're worth clicking.
That's your entire audition.

If your cover doesn't grab attention, the audition's over before it begins.

Your cover isn't decoration; it's a sales conversation.
It tells readers, *"This book belongs here. This book gets you."*
And if it looks off—like it was designed by your cousin using clip art and optimism—readers won't think, *"Oh, how authentic."*
They'll think, *"If the cover looks like this, what's the inside going to be like?"*

You don't need an award-winning design.
You just need a cover that looks like it belongs—and *wins*—in your category.

Take a quick stroll through *Amazon's* top nonfiction charts and you'll notice the pattern: clean typography, strong contrast, and clear emotion.
Look at *Atomic Habits* by *James Clear, Dare to Lead* by *Brené Brown,* or *Start with Why* by *Simon Sinek.*

Each one signals clarity and confidence... instantly recognizable, even from a mobile screen.

That's not luck. That's a design strategy built on category psychology.

Now, compare that to the amateur look: five fonts fighting for dominance, a stock photo of a handshake, and a subtitle that could double as fine print. If your cover looks like that, your book's not "underperforming." It's in hiding.

Here's what separates bestsellers from background noise:

1. ***Visibility loves clarity:*** Clever designs might win awards, but clear titles win clicks. Make it bold, legible, and unmistakable... because on *Amazon*, no one squints to understand your book.

2. ***Visual cues matter:*** Every category has its look. Business books feel focused and confident. Personal development feels bright and energizing. Memoirs feel warm and human. Match your reader's expectations... then elevate them.

3. ***Emotion sells:*** Great covers don't just show what the book is about; they make readers *feel* something. A leadership book should feel empowering. A burnout recovery book should feel safe. A creativity book should feel alive.

4. ***Test before you finalize:*** One of the smartest things an author can do is involve their audience early. Post your title, subtitle, or cover options on social media and ask for honest feedback. You're not just collecting opinions; you're *pre-selling engagement.*

People love to feel part of your success, and when they do, they'll become your loudest advocates at launch.

And here's a quick insider trick:

Shrink your cover down to thumbnail size… or even better, view it on your phone next to similar titles.

If you can still read the title, sense the message, and feel the vibe, you're good.

If it vanishes into the background or looks like a PowerPoint slide from 2009, back to the drawing board.

In professional publishing, we always remind authors: your cover isn't an accessory; it's an asset.

Because on *Amazon* (and all other book retailers), your cover speaks first… and it keeps talking while you're asleep.

A strong cover doesn't just attract clicks.
It builds trust before readers even read your description.
And when your cover looks like it belongs beside the bestsellers
in your space, readers assume you are one.

But a great cover only earns the click.
What happens next depends on the words that greet your reader.

Descriptions That Sell (Without Sounding Like a Sales Page)

Your cover grabs attention.
Your description closes the deal.

Because once readers click your book page, they're asking one question: *"Is this really for me?"*

And that's where most authors blow it.

They treat their *Amazon* description like a formality: a few sentences tossed together in a rush.
The result? A perfectly good book buried under copy that reads like a tax form.

> *Your description isn't a summary.*
> *It's a story with a purpose.*
> *It's your "mini sales conversation"... short, emotional, and focused on helping the reader imagine their transformation.*

If your cover gets the click, your description earns the buy.

Here's the framework smart nonfiction authors use to make that happen:

1. Hook with the Pain Point

Start where your reader already lives... the struggle.
If your book's about leadership, talk about the sleepless nights and impos-

sible decisions.

If it's about productivity, talk about overwhelm, burnout, and that sinking feeling that you're busy all day but achieving nothing.

You wake up exhausted, check your phone before your feet hit the floor, and still end the day wondering what you actually accomplished.

That's not marketing.
That's empathy.

2. Exaggerate the Pain

Don't hold back; lean into it.
Readers buy solutions only after they feel the problem.

You've tried the apps. You've read the quotes. But somehow, you're still stuck—working harder, getting less done, and wondering if everyone else knows something you don't.

Now you've got their attention.

3. Hold Them There

This is where most authors rush in with answers.
Don't. Stay in the pain just a little longer.
Show readers that you truly understand the cost of the problem.

It's not your lack of motivation. It's that no one showed you how to build a system that fits your life, your brain, and your priorities.

Now they're nodding.

You've earned their trust.

4. Introduce the Author as Authority

Once they feel understood, it's time to show why you can help... but *do it in third person.*
This isn't the place for "I've helped thousands" or "I believe in transformation."

Instead, write about the author like a trusted narrator introducing a guide:

Drawing on more than a decade of experience helping professionals simplify their workflow, [Author Name] shows readers how to focus on what matters and finally make consistent progress.

> *Third person builds credibility. It reads like proof, not self-promotion.*

5. Benefits: Paint the Picture of the Future

Now shift from pain to possibility.
Show readers what life looks like after they apply what your book teaches.
Use bullet points... because *Amazon* readers scan before they read.

In this book, you'll discover how to:

- *Stop reacting and start leading your day with clarity*

- *Build habits that actually stick*

- *Reclaim your focus (without deleting every app on your phone)*

- *Feel progress—not burnout—by the end of each week*

Every bullet paints a piece of the future your reader wants.

6. The Call to Action

End with a soft, confident invitation, not hype.

If you're ready to stop spinning your wheels and finally move toward what matters most, this book is your roadmap. Start reading today.

That's it. Clean, emotional, and real.

Your book description shouldn't sound like an ad.
It should sound like *clarity*.

Because when readers feel understood, they don't just buy the book; they trust the author.
And that's the first step toward turning one-time readers into lifelong fans.

Pro Insight:
Before we dive into the next optimization tool, it's worth flagging something you've probably scrolled past on countless book pages... that sleek section labeled "From the Publisher."
It's called A+ Content, and it's one of Amazon's most underused visibility boosters.
In this step, you'll get a quick look at what it does and why it matters.

We'll go deeper into designing and deploying it later, in Step 7, when we build your full optimization and promotion system.

The Secret Weapon: A+ Content (From the Publisher)

If your book description *tells* the story, your *A+ Content shows* it.

Think of it as the movie trailer for your book... the visual story that convinces readers they're in good hands before they even scroll to the reviews.

You've seen *A+ Content* before, even if you didn't realize it.
It's that polished, image-rich section called *"From the Publisher"* sitting quietly between your book details and customer reviews.
It features banners, clean visuals, quotes, and short copy that highlight the book's promise and personality.

Most readers have no idea what *A+ Content* actually is, but they *feel* it.
It's the same subtle credibility cue that used to be exclusive to traditional publishing houses.
When readers see it, they subconsciously *assume, "This book is professionally published."*

And that's the point.

> *A+ Content doesn't just make your listing prettier; it makes it trustworthy.*
> *It bridges the gap between a casual scroll and a confident click.*

Here's why it matters:

1. Most shoppers scan... they don't read long paragraphs.

2. A+ Content turns your listing into an easy visual experience.

3. And *Amazon*'s algorithm quietly indexes some of the text for **internal SEO** — giving you another visibility boost when you use keywords strategically.

So what should you include?

You're not designing for decoration; you're *strategically selling through storytelling.*

- ***A strong hero banner:*** one powerful visual that restates your book's core promise. Something like *"Build the Business Your Book Deserves"* or *"The Proven Path to Publish, Promote, and Monetize."*

- ***Three supporting modules:*** short text sections paired with simple visuals that show transformation. Examples: *"Turn Your Book Into Leads," "Publish Professionally Without Guesswork,"* or *"Monetize Beyond Royalties."*

- **Author credibility strip:** a clean section with your photo, tagline, and one sentence about who you help and how.

Together, these create a smooth visual journey: headline, benefit, credibility, and trust... all in under ten seconds.

Pro Tip:

The same keyword logic you used in your metadata and description applies here too.

Sprinkle those phrases naturally into your A+ text modules. *Amazon* reads them.

It's like giving the algorithm breadcrumbs straight to your book.

And here's the secret most indie authors still don't know:

Adding *A+ Content* makes readers feel like your book comes from a *real publisher*.

It instantly elevates your perceived value... even if you published it yourself.

That's why we call it the "From the Publisher" illusion.

Because in a way, it is. You're publishing like a professional.

A+ Content doesn't just sell the book; it sells confidence.

And confidence is built on consistency.

Timing Tip: You can only set up A+ Content after your book is published and approved on *Amazon*.

So for now, plan ahead. Sketch your headlines, visuals, and messages so you're ready to upload the moment your book goes live.

Once it's published, go straight into KDP (Marketing Tab) and set up your A+ section... even a simple version to start. Then, as your data unfolds (what readers click, what converts, what resonates), keep refining.

We'll revisit A+ optimization again in Step 7, when you'll have real performance insights to work with.

The same message, tone, and keywords that power your visuals should also live in your metadata: the invisible framework that tells *Amazon* exactly who your book is for.

Let's give that framework a tune-up.

The Metadata Makeover

By now, you've probably realized something: success on *Amazon* isn't random.
It's architecture.

Your title, subtitle, description, keywords, and categories are all connected... and the thing holding them together is your **metadata.**

Metadata might sound technical, but really, it's just the digital DNA of your book.
It tells *Amazon* who you are, who your readers are, and why your book matters.

In plain English?
Metadata is how the algorithm decides whether to introduce you to new readers... or ghost you completely.

Most authors don't think about it.
They'll spend months debating cover fonts but never notice their backend keywords are things like *"inspiration"* or *"success."*

Those words are so broad *Amazon* doesn't even blink.

Think of metadata as your book's elevator pitch... but you're pitching it to a robot that reads 12 million books a day.
That robot doesn't care about poetry. It cares about clarity.

Here's what really matters:

1. Your Title and Subtitle

Your title is the hook.

Your subtitle is the promise.

Together, they should tell readers exactly what they'll get... no guessing required.

Let's play a quick round of "Guess the Book."

If your title is *Phoenix Rising,* what's it about?

Could be productivity. Could be divorce recovery. Could be a fantasy novel about a bird on fire.

That's the problem: no clarity, no clicks.

Now look at *Deep Work: Rules for Focused Success in a Distracted World.*

Title: emotional hook.

Subtitle: clear benefit.

That's the model.

A keyword-rich subtitle does half your marketing for you. It tells *Amazon*—and your reader—exactly what the book delivers.

Because clarity isn't just good writing; it's good positioning.

2. Backend Keywords

Behind the scenes, *Amazon* gives you seven keyword boxes.

These are your secret map... your chance to tell the system all the phrases readers might use to find your book.

But here's what most authors do wrong: they repeat words from their title or stuff the boxes with every buzzword they can think of.
That's like whispering in seven different directions at once... *no one hears you clearly.*

Instead, use those spaces to capture long, natural phrases that sound like how people actually search:

- Instead of "leadership," use "how to lead a team remotely."

- Instead of "mindset," use "how to stop negative thinking."

- Instead of "productivity," use "focus strategies for entrepreneurs."

That's how you teach *Amazon* who your readers really are.

3. Series and Contributors

If your book is part of a series, that's metadata gold.
It helps *Amazon* connect your titles together... creating automatic cross-promotion between your own books.

Same goes for contributors, editors, and co-authors.
Consistent listings make *Amazon* see you as a professional brand, not a one-off hobbyist.

In professional publishing, we always remind authors that *Amazon's* memory is long.
The more consistent your details, the more the algorithm trusts you.

4. Description Fields and A/B Testing

Your *Amazon* description isn't a one-time upload; it's a living, testable piece of marketing.

Smart authors experiment.
They tweak headlines, rearrange bullet points, or update testimonials to see what increases conversions.

Every small change gives *Amazon* new data to learn from.
It's the same principle used by digital marketers, just applied to your book page.

If one version keeps readers scrolling and another doesn't, *Amazon* notices. And when your page performs better, your book ranks higher.

That's not luck. That's feedback.

Metadata isn't glamorous. It's not the stuff that gets likes on Instagram. But it's what makes your book *findable, clickable, and buyable.*

And when it's done right, it works quietly in the background... introducing you to readers while you sleep.

So before you chase the next marketing trend, ask yourself:
Have I taught Amazon who my book is for?

Because clarity doesn't just help readers.
It helps algorithms, too.

And when both understand your message... visibility stops being a mystery.

Once your visuals and *A+ Content* tell a compelling story, there's one vital element left... *you*. Readers don't just buy books; they buy into authors. Give them a place to meet the person behind the pages.

Build Your Author Page Before You Launch

Once your book listing is ready (and approved)—the cover looks sharp, the description pops, and the price says "professional"—there's one last step before you hit the gas on promotion:
build your *Amazon Author Page*.

Because your Author Page isn't just a profile; it's your storefront inside the world's biggest bookstore.
When someone clicks your name under your book title, this is where they land.
And what they see there determines whether they think, "One-book wonder" or "Author with a future."

Timing Tip:
You can only set up your Author Page after your book is published and approved in Amazon's system.
So for now, plan for it.
Draft your author bio, choose your photo, and decide what story your page should tell.
Once your book goes live, log in to *Author Central* and build it right away... it's the quickest way to make your author brand feel official.

What Your Author Page Does for You

Your Author Page is Amazon's version of a personal website, except it lives where the buyers already are.

It allows you to:

- ***Show all your books in one place.*** Kindle, paperback, hardcover, and audiobook—all versions neatly displayed.

- ***Add a professional bio and author photo.*** Readers want to know the face and story behind the words.

- ***Gain followers.*** When readers click "Follow," Amazon notifies them of future releases automatically... for free.

This isn't just an author bio page. It's your brand hub inside the world's biggest book marketplace.

How to Set It Up (and Get It Right)

1. Go to author.amazon.com and create your *Author Central* account.

2. Claim your book... Amazon will verify you as the author.

3. Add your bio (written in your natural voice: short, warm, and personal)... and in *third person*.

4. Upload a high-quality photo that matches your brand style.

5. If you have multiple books, make sure each one is linked—it can take up to 72 hours to sync.

Done right, this takes less than an hour, but it's one of the most valuable pieces of real estate you own on *Amazon*.

Pro Tips for Standing Out

- Write your bio like you're introducing yourself to a podcast audience... friendly, not formal.

- Always write it in *third person* ("[Author Name] helps entrepreneurs publish and promote their books") rather than "I." It sounds more professional and aligns with how readers and retailers expect to see author bios.

- Mention your mission or the transformation your readers can expect across your work.

- Add a line that subtly ties your books together ("Through his/her books and coaching, [Author Name] helps experts turn their ideas into income").

- Update it regularly with new releases, media mentions, or awards. Your Author Page should evolve as your brand grows.

And yes, your Author Page has its own analytics dashboard inside *Author Central*. Use it. You'll see page views, book performance data, and even which of your titles are getting the most attention.

It's not just about looking professional; it's about owning your corner of Amazon's ecosystem.

> *Once readers finish your book, the first thing they click is your name.*
> *Make sure where they land tells the same story as your book does—that you're here to stay.*

Your Author Page closes the publishing loop... it turns browsers into followers and followers into future buyers. By the time you finish this step, your book isn't just discoverable; it's clickable, credible, and conversion-ready.

Own Your ISBNs Like a Pro

Before you hit *Publish*, take a moment for a few professional must-dos that separate amateurs from authors who mean business.

When you publish on *Amazon* or *IngramSpark*, you'll be offered a free ISBN.
It's convenient... and also one of the worst shortcuts you can take.

Here's why:
That *"free"* ISBN doesn't actually belong to you. It registers *Amazon* or *IngramSpark* as the publisher of record.

So when bookstores or libraries look up your title, they see them... not you.

That small detail quietly affects your control, distribution, and credibility.

Instead, here's what the pros do:

- Buy your own ISBNs from *Bowker* (in the U.S.) or *Nielsen* (in the U.K.).

- Or, if you're working with a publishing partner, have them assign official ISBNs… one for each format (paperback, hardcover, Kindle, audiobook).

Even Kindle—yes, even though *Amazon* doesn't require an ISBN for eBooks—should have one. It keeps your catalog clean and consistent across platforms.

Owning your ISBNs gives you full control of your publishing rights and ensures your books look like what they are: professionally published assets, not side projects.

Price With Intention

Pricing a book isn't about guessing what feels "fair." It's about *engineering perception.*

Your price tells a story long before your description does. For example, when it comes to *Kindle* pricing…

$0.99 says, *"I'm experimenting."*

$2.99 says, *"I'm self-published."*

$9.99 says, *"I'm professional."*

And free? That says, *"I'm fishing for attention."*

None of these are wrong, but each sends a message.

And the smartest authors choose their message deliberately.

The Psychology of Price

Readers don't think in numbers; they think in meaning.

When someone sees a $2.99 business book sitting next to a $9.99 one, their brain doesn't say, *"Oh, great deal!"* It says, *"Why is this one cheaper?"* Because price is a proxy for trust.

We instinctively associate higher price with higher authority—especially in nonfiction. The $9.99 book feels established, confident, and credible. The $2.99 book might be equally valuable, but it signals uncertainty.

In other words, you're not pricing a product. You're pricing *perception.*

Anchor Pricing: Framing the Choice

When you set your price, you're not competing against "every book." You're competing against whatever else your reader sees on the same screen.

Amazon automatically shows price comparisons—Kindle vs. paperback vs. audiobook—side by side. That means each version of your book influences how the others *feel.*

Here's how professionals use that to their advantage:

- ***Price your Kindle edition slightly lower*** to encourage impulse buys and ad conversions.

- ***Price your paperback higher*** to anchor perceived value. (If

Kindle is \$6.99 and paperback is \$15.99, the eBook suddenly feels like a steal.)

- ***Add an audiobook later*** to elevate the whole catalog—even readers who don't buy it will register the higher anchor price as credibility.

Smart pricing isn't about maximizing profit per copy. It's about positioning your book as *worth buying*.

The Launch Strategy

During launch, your goal isn't just to make money; it's to generate momentum.

That's why many publishers use *strategic price drops* or *free Kindle promos* for a short window. The point isn't to devalue your book; it's to feed Amazon's algorithm with downloads, reviews, and activity.

Once the algorithm starts connecting your title to search behavior ("people who bought *X* also bought *you*"), your discoverability rises.

But here's the catch:
Promos only work when your listing already converts.
Discounts won't fix a weak page; they'll just expose it faster.

So, never use price as a crutch for poor presentation.
Use it as a lever for timing.

Launch lower to accelerate visibility.
Then raise it to match your brand's authority.

Nothing says "bestseller" like a price that climbs after people start buying.

When the Data Comes In

Just like your keywords and A+ visuals, pricing isn't a one-and-done decision.

Once your ads start running and you've got data rolling in, watch how readers respond:

- **High clicks but low sales?** Price may feel too high for the perceived value.

- **Steady conversions but low ROI?** Raise it slowly... $1 increments can make a big difference.

- **Flat performance?** Test small price experiments during quiet weeks to see if your conversion rate changes.

Amazon tracks price elasticity automatically. When your book starts selling more at a particular point, the algorithm favors that sweet spot.

So don't set your price and forget it; *study it.*

The Perception of Confidence

Ultimately, your price is a reflection of your brand's self-image.

If your goal is to position yourself as an authority, price like one.

A confident price tells readers, *"This is worth your attention."*

You can always lower a price strategically, but you can't easily recover from launching too low.

So choose intentionally, test intelligently, and adjust confidently.

Because price doesn't just affect sales; it shapes how the world sees your value.

Pro Insight: Publish Kindle First

Before you rush to publish all formats, start with *Kindle*.

Here's why:

Your Kindle edition gives you flexibility. You can test your title, subtitle, cover, and description live on Amazon... and tweak them based on real reader data before you commit to print.

Once your book's performance metrics (clicks, conversions, and ad response) look strong, *then* publish your paperback and hardcover editions.

Those versions are permanent (i.e., the title and the subtitle will be locked in), but *Kindle* lets you learn what works first.

You'll go deeper into this strategy in Step 7... when we cover how to use *Kindle* as your testing ground before finalizing your print editions.

The Book Posture Report: See What's Really Holding Your Book Back

If your book's already live on *Amazon* but it's not performing the way you hoped, you're not alone.
Most authors don't fail because their ideas are weak; they fail because their *positioning* is.

The most common problems hide in plain sight: mismatched categories, unclear metadata, weak keywords, or descriptions that don't connect emotionally.
Even great books can disappear when those fundamentals are off.

That's why in professional publishing, we use what's called a *Book Posture Report*: a quick diagnostic check that reveals where your listing might be quietly underperforming.

Think of it like a fitness assessment for your book's visibility.
You'll see what's strong, what's lagging, and what tweaks could instantly improve your discoverability.

It's free to request, and it's designed specifically for authors who've already launched but feel stuck in "invisible mode."
You can access it here:
https://authority-publishing.com/republish-manuscript

This isn't a sales pitch; it's a reality check.
A professional mirror for your book's presence on *Amazon,* so you can see exactly what's holding it back *before* spending another cent on ads or marketing.

Because sometimes, the smallest corrections—a subtitle rewrite, a keyword shift, a category change—make the biggest difference.

And the best part?
Once you know what's off, fixing it is simple.

So before you move on to promotion strategies, make sure your book's posture is right.
Because even the best marketing in the world can't help a listing that's standing crooked.

Once your foundation's strong, everything else—promotion, visibility, monetization—starts working faster and easier.
Let's wrap this step up and look at how all the pieces fit together.

Bring It Home

Let's be honest: *Amazon* doesn't sell the best books.

It sells the best-positioned ones.

You could write the next *Think and Grow Rich*, but if your keywords, categories, or cover are off... nobody will ever find it.

Visibility isn't luck. It's structure.

Every title, subtitle, description, and metadata field is a brick.

Stack them right, and *Amazon* becomes your most loyal salesperson.

Stack them wrong, and your book becomes the internet's best-kept secret.

Before you jump into promotion, pause for a quick gut-check:

- *Can readers actually find my book when they search for their problem?*

- *Would I click on my own listing if I saw it beside ten others?*

- *Do my title, subtitle, and cover make it instantly clear what my book delivers?*

If even one of those made you hesitate... great. That's your next fix.

Because every small improvement you make sends a new signal to *Amazon*:

"This book belongs with those readers."

And when *Amazon* believes you, it does the heavy lifting... quietly putting your book in front of the people who need it most.

That's the real game.

You're not just publishing a book.
You're training an algorithm to introduce you to the world.
And once it learns, it doesn't stop.

So optimize once. Refine often.
And watch your book do what it was built to do:
not just sit there, but *be found, be read, and be remembered.*

Step 6: Seed Monetization Inside Your Book

The Book Is the Beginning, Not the End

On Monday, Maya hit "Publish," took a victory photo with her book, and watched the first-week sales roll in.

By Friday, the dashboard went quiet. No emails. No replies. No next steps. Just... silence.

A month later she added three quiet invitations to her chapters: a checklist here, a visual map there, and one short video walkthrough. Nothing hypey, just helpful.

That's when the notes started:
"Downloaded the worksheet!"
"Booked a call."
"Just joined the community."

Publishing wasn't the finish line. It was the first handshake... and the first invitation.

Your book isn't a trophy for the shelf. It's a handshake. A "nice to meet you." The start of a conversation that continues long after the final page.

When someone buys your book, they're literally paying to spend hours with your voice. You've earned their attention, curiosity, and maybe even a bit of trust. That's rare. Most marketers would sell their left AirPod for that kind of access.

But if your book ends without giving readers a *next step,* you've missed one of the most valuable opportunities you'll ever have.

You're not trying to sell them something; you're keeping the connection alive. Inviting them to learn more. To stay in touch. To keep the conversation going.

Because when someone finishes your book and thinks, *"I wish I could learn more from this person,"* that's not the end of your story; that's your opening line.

Don't just sell books. Let your book sell you.

Every Page Is a Doorway

Most authors treat their book like a closed room instead of a hallway.

They lock the door behind the reader, pat themselves on the back, and think, *"Well, that's done."*

But if your book doesn't give readers a way to walk further into your world—your ideas, your email list, your business—you've basically closed the door right after inviting them in.

Every page is a chance to open a doorway.

Not with flashing "BUY MY COURSE" signs, but with small, natural invitations that make readers think, *"I'd love to see that in action."*

You've probably seen this done well in books that say things like:

"Want to see how this framework works? Download the visual map at..."
"Grab the checklist that goes with this chapter at..."
"Join the private community where we're applying these ideas at..."

It's not selling. It's serving.

These micro-CTAs (calls to action) turn your book from a monologue into a guided experience.
Each one gives your reader something valuable right when they care most about it.

Placement matters too. Don't hide your best CTA in the acknowledgments where only your mom will see it. Sprinkle them where engagement peaks... early in the introduction, at key transitions, or right after a strong teaching moment.

The goal is subtlety. Readers should feel helped, not hunted.

When someone's deep in a chapter and thinking, *"I love how this person explains things,"* that's your cue to hand them a quiet key and whisper, *"There's more where that came from."*

Every page should lead somewhere... not to a sale, but to a step
that builds trust.
That's how your book stops being a product and starts becoming
a pathway.

The Rule of Relevance

Ever been in a conversation where someone suddenly pitches you something that has nothing to do with what you were just talking about?

You're sharing a story about your dog, and suddenly they're selling crypto. That's what a bad book CTA feels like.

If you want your reader to take the next step, your invitation has to match the moment they're in.

Imagine you've just spent five pages teaching how to design a great client onboarding system. The worst thing you could do next is say, *"By the way, join my 10K Mastermind."*

The right move? Offer something that extends what they just learned:

"Want my exact onboarding checklist? Grab it free at..."
"Need the sample script I use with new clients? Download it here..."
"I recorded a short video showing how this works in action... you can watch it at..."

A relevant CTA feels like part of the lesson. It adds instant value right when the reader needs it most. You're not asking for something; you're offering something useful.

Think of it like dessert after a great meal. You don't need to convince anyone; they already want more.

That's the power of relevance: it turns marketing into momentum. When your offer flows naturally from the content, it doesn't feel like an interruption. It feels like a favor.

Readers who feel helped will almost always follow you to the next page, the next link, or the next product... because you've already earned their trust.

The rule is simple: never drop a CTA that breaks the reader's rhythm. When you break relevance, you break connection.

Lines, Not Walls

Most people hear the phrase "sales funnel" and picture something slimy... a trapdoor that drops readers straight into an upsell.

Relax. You're not building a funnel. You're drawing lines.

Lines connect. Walls divide.

A line says, *"If you liked this, here's where it continues."*
A wall says, *"Stop right there... hand over your email before you can move forward."*

Readers shouldn't feel extracted from your book and dumped into a marketing sequence. They should feel invited, like you're letting them in on something special.

These are your *value pathways:* soft bridges that guide people from reading your words to experiencing your world.

It could be a free resource that expands on a chapter concept, a short bonus video that shows the process in action, or a simple *"want to go deeper?"* checklist.

Whatever form it takes, the tone should always say, *"Here's something useful... take it if it helps."*

No countdown timers. No "limited spots available." No all-caps warnings about missing out.

This isn't *click-here-or-else* marketing. It's *come hang out if you liked the vibe.*

The best authors don't build funnels; they build friendships. Once a reader trusts you, following a link isn't a transaction; it's a continuation.

So draw lines. Leave trails. Create bridges.

The goal isn't to trap people in your world. It's to make it so valuable they never want to leave.

Smart CTAs Without Sounding Sleazy

Most book calls-to-action sound like they were written by a used car dealer after too much coffee.

"Click NOW before it's too late!"
"Spots are vanishing faster than my will to live!"

Easy there... it's a book, not a Black Friday sale.

Readers don't want hype. They want help.

A smart CTA feels like part of the conversation, not a commercial break. It sounds like this:

"Want the worksheet that goes with this chapter? Grab it free at…"
"See the full visual map for this framework at…"
"Join the private discussion where readers share how they're applying this step at…"

Each one flows naturally from what came before. It doesn't interrupt the story; it continues it.

The tone? Always friendly. Never desperate.

When your content delivers real value, people *want* to stay connected. You don't need to push; you just need to make it easy.

Think of your CTAs as customer service, not sales. You're saying, *"If this helped, here's where you can get more."*

The best non-fiction authors—the ones quietly building businesses from a single book—all follow the same rule: *give before you ask.*

Their CTAs feel like gifts, not grabs.

You're not pushing readers to do something for *you*. You're inviting them to do something that benefits *them*.

When your call to action genuinely helps—when it makes life easier, faster, or clearer—you don't need pressure tactics. You just need clarity.

Write CTAs that sound like a friend texting you a helpful link, not a marketer chasing a quota.

And remember the golden test: *if you'd cringe hearing it out loud, delete it.*

But even the best-designed pathways won't matter if your book never reaches enough of the right people.

Reader Seeding: Why Pathways Only Work If Readers Arrive

Most authors believe books sell because of algorithms.
They don't.
Books sell because *people talk*.

Publishing insiders know this, even if they rarely admit it publicly. The majority of long-term book revenue doesn't come from launch week. It comes months—sometimes years—after publication, once a book has quietly found its way into the right hands and started moving through conversations.

That's not luck.
That's reader seeding.

Reader seeding simply means this:
intentionally getting your book into the hands of the people it was written for... at scale.

Not influencers.
Not random buyers.
Not vanity audiences.

Real readers. Ideal readers. The ones who recognize themselves on the page and feel compelled to pass the book along.

Because that's how momentum is born.

Why Seeding Matters More Than Launch Day

Traditional publishing still makes most of its profit from books that are more than six months old, yet very little effort is put into supporting them past launch. Why? Because publishers already understand something most authors don't: ***Word of mouth is the real distribution engine.***

Algorithms amplify what people already respond to. They don't create belief.

If you publish a great book and don't actively seed it, you're asking Amazon—or social media—to do the job people are supposed to do.
And they won't.

Momentum only starts once enough real readers are exposed to your idea at the same time.

The Seeding Threshold

There is a tipping point where a book starts to carry itself.

From experience and industry data, that number usually sits somewhere between:

- ***1,000 copies:*** the minimum needed to give your book a real chance

- ***20,000 copies:*** enough to know, with confidence, whether the message truly resonates

Below that, it's impossible to tell whether a book failed because of the idea or simply because not enough people ever encountered it.

This is why *"I published my book, and it didn't sell"* is almost always a meaningless statement.

Most books don't fail.
They're never meaningfully seeded.

Why Format Doesn't Matter as Much as You Think

Authors often obsess over whether they should push print, eBook, or audio.
That's the wrong question.

The right question is, *"How many people have encountered the idea?"*

Some readers only consume audio.
Others will only read a physical book.
Very few care about format; they care about relevance.

Your job isn't to pick the "perfect" format.
Your job is to **remove friction** and let readers choose.

Momentum comes from reach, not preference.

The Two-Copy Rule

One of the simplest and most effective seeding strategies is this:
Never give away one copy. Give away two.

Why?

Because a single copy is consumed privately.
A second copy creates intent.

When someone receives an extra book, they instinctively ask themselves,
"*Who do I know who needs this?*"

That moment—when a reader personally recommends your book to someone else—is more powerful than any ad you will ever run.

The book doesn't arrive as a product.
It arrives as a *trusted suggestion*.

That's when word of mouth actually starts.

Seeding Is How You Get "Lucky"

Most breakout books didn't explode because of a perfect launch.
They exploded because the right person encountered the book at the right time.

That only happens if enough books are already circulating.

You cannot predict who will pass your book to a CEO, a podcast host, a community leader, or a decision-maker. But you *can* increase the odds by putting your book in motion.

Reader seeding isn't about forcing virality.
It's about *creating enough surface area* **for serendipity to occur**.

This Is Where Monetization Quietly Begins

Here's the part most authors miss:

> *Reader seeding doesn't just sell books.*
> *It seeds clients, conversations, and opportunities.*

When the right readers encounter your book:

- They don't just buy; they inquire

- They don't just read; they reach out

- They don't just finish; they ask, *"What's next?"*

That's why this book insists on embedding clear, ethical paths inside your content—not aggressive pitches, but logical next steps.

Seeding without monetization is wasted leverage.
Monetization without seeding is premature.

The two must work together.

The Long Game Most Authors Never Play

Marketing a book isn't a one-week event.
It's closer to building a company than launching a product.

The authors who win long-term commit to sustained visibility—not constant noise, but consistent presence.

If you are willing to seed your book steadily over one to two years, something interesting happens:

- Momentum compounds.

- Trust accumulates.

- The book starts opening doors without you pushing it.

That's when the book stops being the product and starts becoming the engine.

The Monetization Pyramid

Here's a wild idea: your book isn't just a book. It's a business funnel in a tuxedo.

Beneath all that storytelling and insight, it quietly does three jobs: builds trust, creates bridges, and drives revenue.

I call this the *Monetization Pyramid.*

At the base are your *Trust Builders...* free, no-pressure offers that say, *"Let's get to know each other."*

- A downloadable checklist or resource

- A short video or email mini-course

- A quiz, toolkit, or companion guide

These cost nothing but curiosity, yet they open the door to real connection.

Move up a level to the *Value Bridges.* This is where readers step deeper into your world... not because you pushed them, but because they *want* to.

- A course that expands on your book's process

- A consultation or strategy session

- A paid community or membership

These are the *"I like what you teach... show me more"* moments.

At the top are your *Revenue Drivers...* your high-value offers that fund your mission and your next book:

- One-on-one coaching or done-for-you services

- Speaking engagements and workshops

- Corporate consulting or licensing deals

Most authors make the mistake of starting here, skipping the trust phase, and going straight for the sale. But nobody buys from strangers.

When your book is designed like a pyramid—each level leading naturally to the next—you never have to "sell." Readers simply climb.

They start with something free that helps them win a small victory. That success builds reader confidence. That confidence sparks curiosity... and curiosity leads to commitment.

Before you know it, they're not just readers; they're clients.

Your book becomes the first step in a human relationship that grows over time.

So stop thinking of monetization as a jump from *reader* to *customer*. Think of it as a gentle ascent: one step, one win, and one value-add at a time.

That's how professionals do it: building a business on the back of a book without ever sounding like they're trying.

Traditional publishing often treats a book like sacred ground: beautifully produced but locked down. Once it's printed, you can't easily update links, embed lead magnets, or guide readers toward your world without getting lost in contracts and editorial rules. That's the tradeoff of working with legacy houses like *Penguin Random House*... they control the product, not you.

Hybrid publishing gives authors something far more valuable: creative and commercial freedom. You own your book's direction, its assets, and the pathways inside it. You can fine-tune your *Amazon* presence, build your reader ecosystem, and weave in CTAs that connect your book directly to your business.

It's the modern author's advantage: the freedom to turn every page into a possibility, every insight into a next step, and every reader into a relationship.

The Golden Rule: Make It Worth Their Time

Let's get one thing straight: if your "freebie" flops, nothing else matters.

You can have the best book, the slickest funnel, and the most charming emails ever written... but if what you give readers first feels like homework or a sales trap, they're gone.

Think about your own inbox. How many times have you downloaded a "free guide" that turned out to be five pages of fluff and a hard pitch? Exactly.

> *The golden rule of book monetization is simple: make it worth their time.*

There's a simple psychology at work here: when you give people real utility without pressure, they naturally lean in. Call it reciprocity or just good manners... useful beats urgent. A clear win today earns you attention tomorrow.

Your reader just spent hours with you. They've laughed at your stories, underlined your advice, and maybe even told a friend about your book. At that moment, they *want* to trust you.

Don't betray that trust by serving up junk.

If you promise a worksheet, make it something they'll actually use. If you offer a video, make it short, sharp, and packed with value... not a 45-minute monologue that feels like a webinar in disguise. And if you create a lead magnet, treat it like your book's little sibling: same tone, same quality, same integrity.

Here's the secret: generosity scales faster than persuasion.

When you give people something genuinely useful, you build emotional equity. They think, *"If the free stuff is this good, imagine what the paid stuff is like."*

That's how you turn a reader into a fan, a fan into a client, and a client into a lifelong advocate.

It's not about manipulation; it's about momentum. Every genuine, helpful interaction adds relationship equity until one day, the reader isn't being sold; they're simply saying *yes* to more of what already worked.

Before you publish any resource, ask yourself one question: *Would I be impressed if I downloaded this?*

If the answer's *no*, fix it until it's *yes*.

Your reader's time is the most expensive currency you'll ever ask for... spend it wisely.

Bring It Home

Writing a great book is hard enough. Turning it into a business engine? That's next level.

The good news: you don't need to be a marketing wizard to make it work. You just need to think like a guide, not a guru.

Your book isn't a finish line; it's an invitation. Every chapter, every story, every insight is a door you quietly leave open for the reader to walk through when *they're* ready.

That's how you build trust that lasts long after launch week.

Before you move on, ask yourself:

- *Does my book give readers a next step that feels natural?*

- *Are my CTAs placed where readers are most engaged, not where I'm most desperate?*

- *Am I offering real value before I ever ask for commitment?*

- *If I were my own reader, would I want to follow the path I've built?*

If you can answer *yes* to those, congratulations... you're already doing what most authors never do.

Because the real goal isn't to close your book with *"The End."* It's to close it with *"What's next?"*

That question—and how you answer it—is where the real monetization begins.

Now let's make sure the right readers actually find those pathways... welcome to Part II: Promote.

Part II: Promote
Visibility Beats Perfection

You did it. You built the book. You've shaped your ideas, nailed your message, and crafted a piece of work that reflects your expertise.
But now comes the moment every author secretly dreads.

You hit publish... and wait.

Silence.

No confetti. No sudden flood of readers. Not even a polite email from Jeff Bezos saying, *"Nice job, champ."*

Because here's the truth every author eventually learns:
Publishing isn't the finish line. It's the starting signal.

The world doesn't automatically line up to read your book just because it exists.
It needs to find it first.

That's what this part is about.

Part I was about building the book.
Part II is about building its audience.

You've created the asset... now it's time to make it move.

Because the best book in the world means nothing if no one sees it.
Visibility beats perfection… every single time.

Think of it this way: you've spent months building a beautiful store—polished floors, perfect lighting, and the product (your book) neatly displayed in the front window.
But if nobody walks in, it doesn't matter how stunning it looks inside.

Promotion is how you open the doors. It's the oxygen that keeps your message alive, the motion that turns your book from a static idea into a living conversation.

And no, it's not about shouting louder or dancing for clicks.
Promotion isn't noise. It's precision.

It's about being found by the right people, in the right places, at the right time… people who don't just want what you wrote, but *need* it.

This is where your book stops being a product and starts becoming a presence.
It's where *Amazon* starts recognizing you as more than another author.
It's where your book begins to build its own gravity… pulling in readers, leads, and opportunities 24/7.

- You'll learn how to build a launch-ready *Amazon* listing that converts casual browsers into buyers.

- You'll see how to drive meaningful traffic that feeds the algorithm instead of confusing it.

- You'll discover how visibility turns into credibility… and how credibility becomes proof that sells your next big idea before you even pitch it.

- And you'll learn how to keep momentum long after launch day, so your book keeps selling while you move on to your next chapter… literally and figuratively.

Think of this part as the ignition switch.
You've built the engine. You've fueled it with purpose and clarity.
Now it's time to turn the key.

Because publishing made you an author…
but promotion makes you known.

You've built the book.
Now, let's make the world notice.

Step 7: Optimize Your Amazon Listing Before You Go to Print

The Post-Publish Pause

YOU HIT *PUBLISH*... AND your book is live. Your name's on *Amazon*, your cover's shining in the *Kindle* store, and it feels like a finish line.

Here's the truth: you've just entered the testing phase.

But before you print a single page, you need to make sure your listing performs in the wild... because publishing isn't the end; it's where optimization starts.

Here's the thing most new authors don't realize: once you publish a print edition, your title, subtitle, author name, and ISBN are *locked forever*. Those can't be changed without creating a brand-new edition, losing your reviews, rank, and history.

But here's the good news: everything else *is flexible.*

Your cover, description, keywords, categories, and pricing can all be tested, refined, and improved inside your Kindle edition before you ever go to print.

That's the pro move.

Smart authors treat *Kindle* like their sandbox: their testing ground for what works.

Because *Kindle* lets you see real buyer behavior: what attracts clicks, what converts to sales, and what quietly falls flat.

So before you publish your paperback or hardcover, you test your *Kindle* edition live on *Amazon*.

You tweak your listing, track the data, and fine-tune the details until you know your packaging is pulling its weight.

And here's a little-known strategy that separates professionals from amateurs:

Start Kindle without an ISBN.

You don't need one yet... *Amazon* gives every *Kindle* book its own unique ASIN (Amazon Standard Identification Number).

That ASIN functions like an internal ID: it identifies your Kindle edition across Amazon's ecosystem.

It's free, automatic, and perfectly fine while you're in testing mode.

Once you've refined your title, subtitle, and cover—and you're confident your listing performs—then you can assign your own ISBN to your *Kindle* and print editions.

That's the version you'll take permanently, with data to back it up.

This isn't hesitation; it's craftsmanship.

Kindle gives you flexibility, freedom, and feedback in real time.

So before you rush into your "final" version, pause.

This is your moment to turn a good listing into a great one... one that's ready to perform before you spend a single dollar on ads or a single cent on print.

Ready? Let's test, refine, and optimize your *Amazon* listing so your print book launches like a pro... not a prototype.

The Psychology of the Window Display

Your book is live.

Whether it's just your *Kindle* edition or your full lineup of formats, you now have something every author dreams of: an *Amazon* listing that lives in the world.

You've just placed your book in the window display of the world's largest bookstore. And every day, readers are walking by.

Imagine standing outside a row of shops.
Some windows sparkle. Others look tired.
One has clean signage and warm lighting that draws you in. Another looks like it hasn't seen a broom since 2009.

Which one would you walk into?

That's *Amazon*.

Except instead of window displays, you've got covers, titles, and descriptions... each one fighting for a split second of attention.

Your *Amazon* listing is the digital face of your book.
It's the moment where a reader decides—often subconsciously—if this

feels worth clicking, reading, or buying.

Readers don't study listings carefully; they react to them instantly.
They're scanning with instinct, not analysis.
And in that moment, three questions determine everything:

1. *Is this for me?*

2. *Can I trust it?*

3. *Do I feel something?*

If the answer is *no* to any of those, the scroll continues.

That's the psychology behind your window display... the split-second moment when browsers decide whether to stop or scroll.

Now that your book is live, you can start looking at it through your readers' eyes:

- *Open your listing as if you've never seen it before.*

- *Does your cover stand out among similar titles?*

- *Does your subtitle promise something specific?*

- *Do your first two lines of description pull emotion before information?*

You won't get deep analytics yet (those will come once you start running Amazon Ads), but you can already study how your page feels.
Your sales rank, reviews, and even the absence of clicks tell you something

about how your storefront is being perceived.

This is the author's moment to stop guessing and start observing.
Before, you were designing in the dark. Now, your listing is live in daylight.

So step back. Look at your book as a buyer would.
Your *Amazon* page isn't just a product listing; it's a living first impression.
And the better you understand how readers experience it, the smarter your next refinements will be.

In the next section, we'll zoom in on the most valuable real estate of all...
the "above-the-fold" area: the first thing every reader sees before they ever scroll.
That's where 90% of buying decisions are made... and where small tweaks can change everything.

The Above-the-Fold Effect

When someone lands on your *Amazon* page, they see exactly one thing before scrolling:
the *above-the-fold* area.

That first (top) rectangle of screen space is where first impressions are made... or lost.

Think of it like the end-of-aisle shelf in a bookstore... the spot everyone sees first when they walk past.
You could serve the best espresso in the city, but if people walk by and see dirty tables and an unplugged "Open" sign, they'll keep walking to Starbucks... even if your coffee would've changed their life.

That's the *above-the-fold* effect.

On *Amazon*, that window includes five key elements:

1. ***The cover image:*** your book's face.

2. ***The title and subtitle:*** your handshake.

3. ***The star rating and reviews:*** your book's reputation.

4. ***The price:*** your book's perceived value.

5. ***The first two lines of your description:*** your hook.

Together, those five elements form your *split-second sales pitch*.
They tell readers whether to keep exploring or keep scrolling.

And now that your book is live, your job is to study how each one performs... not with fancy analytics (we'll get there in the next step), but with observation and comparison.

Open your Amazon page on both desktop and mobile.
Then, open three bestselling books in your category.
Compare them side by side.

Ask yourself:

- *Does my cover stand out or blend in?*

- *Is my subtitle immediately clear, or does it need a second read?*

- *Do my first two lines make me feel something, or do they sound like a résumé?*

- *How does my price look next to others... professional or bargain bin?*

- *If I knew nothing about me, would I trust this book?*

Each of those questions points to a small improvement with a big impact.

You don't need data yet to know what feels off.
Your instincts as a reader are already strong... use them.

And here's the professional mindset: every listing can improve.
Even tiny changes—a clearer subtitle, a cleaner thumbnail, a stronger first sentence—can double your click-through rate once you start running ads.

But for now, this is your visual diagnostic.
You're studying your window display through the reader's eyes... seeing what stands out and what disappears into the background, making sure it's ready to be tested at scale.

> *What happens above the fold determines everything that follows.*
> *If you don't stop the scroll, nothing else matters.*

Up next, we'll turn this insight into action... showing you how to use Kindle as your testing ground before you commit your print editions to permanence.

The Kindle Testing Loop (and How to Optimize Whatever's Live)

Whether your *Kindle* edition is brand new or your book is already live in print, this step is all about *testing and refining what readers actually see on Amazon.*

Because here's the truth: publishing is a milestone, not a finish line.
Once your book is out there, your next job isn't just to promote it; it's to **optimize it.**

The difference between a good listing and a great one usually comes down to what happens right now... this phase between "published" and "promoted."

If you're early in the journey and have only launched your *Kindle* edition, congratulations... you have flexibility.
If you're already in print, don't worry... you can still make powerful changes that improve performance.

Let's break it down.

Scenario 1: You're in Kindle-First Mode

Start with your Kindle edition. Publish it without assigning an ISBN yet... Amazon will assign it a temporary ID for testing (the ASIN you learned about earlier). That's all you need while refining your listing.

Once your listing performs well—readers respond to the title, subtitle, and cover—you can assign your ISBN and move on to print with confidence.

Why wait?

Because your title, subtitle, author name, and ISBN are permanent once your print edition goes live.

But your cover, description, categories, keywords, and pricing can be changed freely.

This makes *Kindle* the perfect *testing ground*.

It's low-risk, editable, and fast.

Treat this stage as your live rehearsal... a chance to refine everything before committing to print.

Scenario 2: You're Already in Print

If your book's already out in paperback or hardcover, don't panic... you can still optimize most of your listing.

You just have to know what's *locked* and what's *flexible*.

Locked:

- *Title*

- *Subtitle*

- *Author name*

- *ISBN*

Flexible (and powerful to optimize):

- **Cover design** (you can reupload a new one under the same edition).

- *Description* (you can update or rewrite it anytime).

- *Categories and keywords* (these directly affect visibility).

- *Price* (you can test new pricing points).

- *A+ Content* and *Author Page* (these can evolve anytime).

In short, even if your book's already printed, 80% of your listing is still adjustable.

You can make small changes that drive major results... especially once you start collecting ad data in the next step.

The Four-Step Testing Loop

Regardless of which camp you're in, here's the universal process for optimizing like a pro:

1. *Publish (or review) your live listing.*
   Look at your page the way a reader would... *is it instantly clear, credible, and clickable?*

2. *Gather feedback and early signals.*
   Watch reviews, feedback from readers, or informal comments when you share your link.
   Note what people say about your title, cover, or positioning.

3. *Refine what's flexible.*
   Adjust your description, categories, keywords, cover, or pricing.
   For Kindle-first authors, this is your chance to polish before print.
   For print authors, it's your chance to strengthen what's already

live.

4. ***Reassess and finalize.***

   After a few weeks of updates, revisit your listing.

   Does it feel sharper? Does the message match the market?

   If so, assign or confirm your ISBNs and lock in your print formats with confidence.

The Pro Mindset

The smartest authors don't treat publishing as an endpoint; they treat it as iteration.

They test, observe, and adjust until their book converts readers naturally.

Whether you're in testing mode with *Kindle* or already holding your paperback, the principle is the same:

what gets optimized gets amplified.

Because even the smallest improvement—a stronger first line, a sharper subtitle, a cleaner cover—can make your book twice as clickable once the traffic starts flowing.

Up next, we'll take this mindset even further... learning how to optimize your listing like a pro by refining metadata, keywords, and categories that quietly make or break your discoverability on *Amazon*.

Optimize Your Listing Like a Pro

Now that your book is live—whether it's just *Kindle* or all formats—it's time to think like a professional publisher.

Your listing isn't a static profile. It's a living asset.
And the authors who win on Amazon are the ones who keep tuning it until it performs effortlessly.

Think of your *Amazon* page like a *Formula 1* car: you've built it, you've tested it, and now you're fine-tuning the engine before the race.

Here's how to do it… systematically, simply, and without losing your mind.

1. Fine-Tune Your Metadata

Behind every beautiful *Amazon* listing is a layer of invisible data… your metadata.
It's what tells Amazon *where* to show your book and *who* to show it to.

If you think of your cover and title as your sales team, metadata is your GPS.

Start with your *keywords* and *categories*.
These are your book's search coordinates: the bridge between what readers are typing and what *Amazon* displays.

- *Keywords:* choose phrases that match your reader's intent ("book marketing for coaches," "how to publish a business book," "turn your expertise into a book").
  You can adjust these anytime in your KDP dashboard.
  Keep refining based on what you learn once ads go live (covered in Step 8).

- *Categories:* make sure your book sits where it can actually rank.

Avoid broad categories like "Business" or "Self-Help."

Pick narrower subcategories where your book can stand out... "Small Business Marketing," "Writing Skills," or "Coaching & Mentoring."

Metadata isn't glamorous, but it's leverage.

Every tweak here teaches *Amazon* who your readers are... and every correct signal increases your organic visibility.

Pro Insight: Your Manuscript Is Never Locked

Most authors think that once their book is published, their manuscript is set in stone. It's not.

You can update and reupload a new file anytime—Kindle or print—without it counting as a new edition.

This means your *content* can evolve with your *visibility strategy*.

One of the smartest moves you can make before you start promoting is to revisit your manuscript and include a few high-relevance, high-traffic keywords in natural places... especially:

- The Table of Contents (Amazon's "Look Inside" scans this).

- The first few pages of the introduction or foreword.

Amazon's algorithms read the text inside your book... not just your metadata. So adding relevant terms organically in those visible sections strengthens your discoverability without changing your message.

Updating your manuscript for relevance isn't rewriting your book; it's reinforcing it.

2. Refresh Your Description

Your book description isn't a one-time upload; it's a living sales page.

You can update it anytime through KDP or Author Central.
Use what you've learned so far—early reviews, reader feedback, or questions people keep asking—to make it sharper and more relevant.

A few power moves:

- Start your first two lines with empathy and curiosity... something that makes the reader *feel seen.*

- Break long paragraphs into shorter, scan-friendly lines.

- Add a call to action that matches reader intent (*"Get your copy and start building your authority today"*).

- Always preview how it looks on desktop and mobile... short sentences sell better on small screens.

Formatting reminder:
Amazon supports simple HTML in descriptions (<b>, <i>, <br>, <ul>, <li>).
Use these lightly to make your copy easy to read, not to decorate.

3. Revisit Your Visuals

Even if your book is already in print, your cover and *A+ Content* are fair game for refinement.

If your listing feels flat compared to others in your niche, consider updating your visuals.

You can reupload a new *Kindle* or paperback cover at any time... same ISBN, same listing.

If your *A+ Content* (the *"From the Publisher"* visuals) is already live, revisit it after a few weeks of feedback. Does it match your brand tone and speak to your target reader? Are the visuals and callouts reinforcing trust? Make sure it aligns with what's resonating most in your other marketing.

Your *A+ Content* is the emotional proof section... the visual reassurance that your book delivers what your title promises.

4. Adjust Pricing with Purpose

Your price is more than a number; it's feedback. Once your *Kindle* or print edition has been live a few weeks, test small adjustments and watch how readers respond.

If sales are slow but clicks are strong, try a slight price drop. If buyers are consistent and reviews are positive, raise the price by a dollar or two to align with similar professional titles.

Amazon's system notices steady conversions... and consistent sales at a slightly higher price often strengthen your ranking.

5. Keep It in Motion

The biggest myth in publishing is that once your book is live, you're done.

The truth: every great book on *Amazon* is continuously evolving behind the scenes.

Authors who treat their listing like a living experiment—checking data, testing covers, refining descriptions—are the ones whose books keep selling years after launch.

Schedule a monthly or quarterly "listing check."
Review your metadata, price, visuals, and description.
Ask, *Does this still reflect the best version of my book?*

Because optimization isn't extra work; it's how you future-proof your results.

The Takeaway

Publishing once makes you an author.
Optimizing continuously makes you a brand.

Every change you make now—from your keywords to your visuals—builds momentum for what comes next: driving targeted traffic to your optimized, ready-to-convert listing.

Up next, we'll wrap up this step with your final pre-promotion checklist… ensuring your page is polished, synced, and ready to perform before we start sending the crowd in.

Build It Before You Boost It

Take a breath.

Your book is live.

Your *Amazon* listing is built, refined, and finally starting to look like it belongs among the pros.

You've optimized what you can, tested what matters, and learned how to see your page through your reader's eyes.

Now comes the last pre-promotion checkpoint: the moment that separates amateurs from professionals.

Because amateurs hit *Publish* and immediately start shouting about their book on social media, hoping someone hears.
Professionals pause.
They make sure every element of their window display can convert... because once the spotlight hits, every detail shows.

That pause isn't hesitation; it's strategy.

By now, your entire *Amazon* presence—from your *A+* visuals to your Author Page—should tell one clear story. This is your brand ecosystem on *Amazon*. Keep it polished and consistent before you send new readers its way.

Here's your quick pre-promotion checklist:

- ***Cover:*** Eye-catching and professional... It looks great on desktop and mobile.

- ***Title & Subtitle:*** Still clear, relevant, and benefit-driven... the same test you passed back in Step 5, now confirmed in the wild.

- ***Description:*** Polished, formatted, emotionally engaging.

- ***Keywords & Categories:*** Focused and discoverable.

- ***Price:*** Confident, aligned with your market.

- ***Author Page:*** Connected and consistent with your brand. Check that your bio, photo, and linked books are current... small updates here can boost reader trust.

- ***A+ Content:*** Visual, credible, and current.

- ***Formats Linked:*** *Kindle*, paperback, and hardcover properly synced under one listing.

Once those boxes are ticked, you're ready for real traffic.

Your page isn't a placeholder anymore; it's a *conversion engine.*

Optional Step: Get a Complimentary Book Posture Report

If you're not entirely sure whether your *Amazon* listing is ready for traffic, you're not alone.

Even seasoned authors second-guess their titles, covers, or descriptions before they promote.

That's why we created the *Book Posture Report*: a free, personalized audit of your Amazon listing that highlights what's strong, what's missing, and how to position your book for higher visibility before launch.

It's like a professional tune-up before you hit the gas.

You can request yours at https://authority-publishing.com/republish-manuscript and get clear, actionable feedback within a few days.

No pressure, no pitch... just insight from people who've optimized dozens of *Amazon* bestsellers before you.

Make sure your book is standing tall before you start sending readers its way.

Note: *We're offering this service only to non-fiction books.*

And here's the truth that separates hobbyists from professionals:

Publishing once makes you an author.

Optimizing before promotion makes you a strategist.

You've done the hard part: turning your listing into something that earns attention before it ever pays for it.

From here on, your book doesn't just exist. It performs.

Next, in *Step 8: Drive Traffic Where It Matters*, we'll flip the switch. You'll learn how to bring targeted readers straight to your newly optimized listing, use ads and organic strategies to feed Amazon's algorithm, and finally see your book gain the visibility it deserves.

Because you've already built it.

Now it's time to boost it and...watch it move.

Bring It Home

You've reached the quiet checkpoint most authors skip... the place between publishing and promoting. It's where good books become great performers.

Instead of rushing for visibility, you built readiness. You fine-tuned every piece of your *Amazon* presence until it earned the right to be promoted. That's what professionals do: they don't push harder; they prepare smarter.

Now look at your listing through a reader's eyes. *Does it feel clear? Credible? Compelling?* If the answer is *yes*, you've already done what 90% of authors never will: *you've tested before you boosted.*

Next, in Step 8, we'll take everything you've refined here and give it reach... turning the traffic switch on and letting your book perform in the spotlight it deserves.

Step 8: Drive Traffic Where It Matters

You Can't Sell a Secret

MOST AUTHORS TREAT THEIR books like state secrets.

They publish, whisper a quiet *"it's live"* to the universe, post once on Facebook, and then... wait.

As if Jeff Bezos himself is somewhere in a control room scanning ISBNs for hidden brilliance.

Spoiler: he's not.

Amazon doesn't reward silence.

And yet, most authors act like their books are in a witness protection program. No traffic. No visibility. No buyers.

It's the equivalent of opening a beautiful bookstore in the desert... then wondering why nobody's walking in.

The truth? You can't sell a secret.

Visibility beats perfection every single time.

Earlier, you learned how to build a listing that converts. Now we're shifting gears... from preparing your book to performing with it.

You could have the most beautifully written book in your category—stunning A+ visuals, a hypnotic title, and a description that makes Hemingway weep—but if no one sees it, it's just digital wallpaper.

And here's the part most authors miss: it's not about *more* traffic. It's about *meaningful* traffic.

You don't need millions of random visitors. You need the right readers: the ones already holding their credit cards, scrolling Amazon at midnight, and thinking, *"That's exactly what I've been looking for."*

Everything you've done up to this point—your cover, keywords, categories, and description—was about getting your listing ready.
Now it's time to bring people to it.

But not just *any* people.

Because shouting louder doesn't help if you're shouting in the wrong direction.

Most authors fall into two camps:

1. **_The Social Media Sprinklers:_** posting links everywhere, begging for likes, tagging friends, and hoping someone's aunt in Nebraska buys a copy.

2. **_The Digital Hermits:_** allergic to promotion, convinced that "good books find their readers." (Technically true... right after those readers find someone else's ad.)

Both are wrong.

Traffic isn't about noise. It's about direction.

And this chapter is about sending your traffic where it actually counts: your *Amazon* listing.

Because that's where the buying intent lives.
That's where the algorithm listens.
That's where books start to move... and where momentum begins.

Stop Wasting Traffic

If you've ever clicked an author's *"buy my book"* post on social media, chances are you didn't end up where you were supposed to.

Maybe they sent you to their website home page, where you had to play detective just to find the book.
Or maybe it was an opt-in page for a freebie that didn't even mention the book.
Or worse... a broken link to Goodreads.

Every day, authors waste thousands of potential clicks because they send people everywhere *except* the one place that actually matters: *Amazon*.

Let's be clear: your Amazon listing isn't just another link.
It's the digital equivalent of standing in front of the world's busiest bookstore... right next to the checkout counter.

When someone lands there, they're already in buying mode.
Their credit card is saved. Their address is stored. Their thumb is twitching over the "Buy Now" button.

Why on earth would you send them anywhere else?

Yet, time and again, authors dilute their traffic by spreading it thin across platforms that don't sell books.

"But my website has my whole brand!"
Sure... but your website doesn't have one-click checkout, verified reviews, or Amazon's magical "Customers Also Bought" section that keeps you visible for weeks.

"But I want to grow my email list first!"
Right idea. Wrong order.
First, let Amazon do what Amazon does best: sell books.

Because every visit to your listing counts twice.

It's not just a potential sale; it's a signal.
Each time someone clicks, reads, or buys, Amazon's algorithm takes notes. It says, *"Hmm, people searching for 'business growth mindset' seem to like this one. Let's show it to more of them."*

That's the difference between spraying traffic everywhere and focusing it where it multiplies.

Think of *Amazon* like a self-feeding ecosystem. The more relevant traffic you drive there, the more *Amazon* learns who your book is for... and the more it promotes you for free.

So before you worry about your next landing page or 17-step funnel, start by fixing your traffic leaks.

Replace every generic "buy" link in your posts, emails, and profiles with one destination: *your Amazon page.*

That's it.

Simple. Focused. Profitable.

Traffic without purpose isn't marketing; it's just motion.
And motion without direction gets ignored.

How the Amazon Algorithm Thinks

Earlier, we optimized for how Amazon's search system finds your book.
Now let's look at what happens once real readers start clicking and buying.

If Amazon were a person, it wouldn't be your chatty, creative friend. It would be a data nerd—quiet, observant, and creepily good at noticing patterns.

It doesn't care about your story, your design, or how long you spent choosing the right shade of blue for your cover.
Amazon cares about one thing: *behavior.*

Clicks.
Conversions.
Consistency.

Every time someone searches, clicks, or buys, Amazon's algorithm takes notes like an obsessive detective with a clipboard.

It's not judging your art. It's watching your math.

Think of it this way: Amazon's goal isn't to promote *your* book. It's to promote books that make *itself* more money... titles that people are most likely to buy.

That means if your book converts well—people click, linger, buy, and leave happy reviews—*Amazon* rewards you by showing your book to more of the same kind of shoppers.

It's basically saying, *"Hey, this one keeps people buying. Let's serve it again."*

Now, here's where it gets interesting: the algorithm doesn't just track sales. It tracks **signals.**

- *Impressions* show your book appeared in search results.

- *Clicks* show your title, cover, and price caught someone's eye.

- *Conversions* show your listing delivered on its promise.

- *Reviews* show buyers were happy enough to recommend it.

Each signal fuels your visibility engine.

The stronger your signals, the more the algorithm trusts your book as a *reliable performer...* and the higher it climbs in search and recommendation slots.

Amazon's logic is simple:
Books that sell get seen more.
Books that don't... quietly disappear.

Think of it like a bartender.

If everyone keeps ordering the same drink, what does the bartender do?
They stock more of it, feature it, and tell new customers, *"You've got to try this one… it's popular."*

That's exactly how *Amazon* works. It keeps "serving" what people keep "ordering."

So when you drive *qualified* traffic—people already interested in your topic—you're not just making a sale.
You're training the bartender.

Every click, every sale, every review teaches Amazon who to show your book to next.

And that's where the next section comes in: how to feed Amazon the right data through the most powerful lever authors have… *Amazon Ads.*

> *If you can show the algorithm who your buyers are, it'll spend the rest of its life helping you find more of them.*

The Power of Amazon Ads

Let's get this out of the way first:
Amazon Ads are not a slot machine.
They're a microscope.

Most authors treat them like Vegas… toss in a few bucks, hope for a miracle, and walk away muttering about "luck" when nothing happens.
But the pros?

They treat ads like data labs.

Because that's what Amazon PPC (Pay-Per-Click) really is... a front-row seat inside the algorithm's brain.

Every ad you run generates real-time intel: what keywords trigger your book, which covers grab attention, and which audiences actually buy.

And here's what most authors miss... Amazon Ads don't charge you for visibility; they charge you for clicks.
That means every impression your ad earns before someone clicks is *free marketing.*

Sounds great, right?
Not always.

If your ad racks up a mountain of impressions but nobody clicks, Amazon takes it as a sign that your book isn't catching attention... and quietly stops showing it.

So don't celebrate free impressions unless they're leading to the *right* clicks.
Because in Amazon's world, *CTR is the currency of relevance*.

It's not just about selling more books; it's about learning *why* they sell.
When you understand that, you stop guessing.
You stop saying, *"I think my readers are mid-career entrepreneurs,"* and start saying, *"I know 38-year-old consultants in the U.S. click my ad when they search 'build authority through a book' and buy within two days."*

That's not intuition. That's data.

And in publishing, data beats hope every single time.

Here's how it works in plain English:

You pay Amazon a small amount each time someone clicks your ad. In return, Amazon puts your book right where your dream readers are already searching... the search bar and competitor listings.

You can start with two main campaign types:

- ***Automatic Campaigns:*** You tell Amazon your budget and let its AI go fishing for keywords and placements that convert. It's like hiring a smart intern to test every combination for you.

- ***Manual Campaigns:*** Once you have data from the automatic phase, you take the wheel. You pick the exact keywords, phrases, and categories that produced results—and double down.

Then there are your *ad formats*:

1. ***Sponsored Products:*** These are your bread-and-butter ads... the "you might also like" placements under other books. They're also the most powerful because they give you detailed keyword and search term data. You can see exactly which phrases triggered your ad, which competitor books drove clicks, and whether your book converted after being shown alongside another title. That's gold. *Sponsored Product Ads* are where you gather the clearest insights to guide every future campaign.

2. ***Sponsored Brands:*** These create a mini-banner with your author name, tagline, or featured book. They were once limited to authors with three or more titles, but Amazon now allows Sponsored Brand campaigns even if you have just one or two books.

It's a simple way to boost visibility and build your author brand alongside your product ads.

3. ***Lockscreen Ads:*** Ideal for Kindle books. They appear on devices before a reader even unlocks the screen—prime real estate for impulse clicks.

But here's the part most authors miss:
The real win isn't the sale. It's the *intel*.

When someone clicks your ad and buys your book, *Amazon* knows exactly which keyword, audience, and phrase triggered that purchase.
That keyword then climbs your *organic rankings*.

Suddenly, your book appears naturally for those same searches... even when you're not paying for ads.

You've just fed the algorithm the right data.

That's why running Amazon Ads isn't optional anymore; it's part of building discoverability.

It's how you teach the system who loves your book so it can keep serving it to them again and again.

And unlike most ad platforms, *Amazon* doesn't waste your budget showing your book to people with zero buying intent.
Everyone on Amazon is already there to *buy*.

That's the beauty of it.

When you play your cards right, Amazon Ads don't just drive sales; they create visibility loops.
The system starts recommending you more because you've proven that readers respond.

So yes, you're paying for clicks, but what you're really building is momentum.

Up next, we'll look at how to read that data like a pro... and how to know whether your ads (and your listing) are actually doing their job.

Reading the Right Data

Here's where most authors panic.

They open their Amazon Ads dashboard, see a wall of numbers—impressions, CTR, CPC, ACoS—and suddenly regret that C-minus in high school math.

Relax. You don't need to be a data scientist. You just need to know what to look for.

Think of your ad dashboard like a doctor's report. Each metric tells you something about the health of your listing.
You're not trying to memorize every number; you're looking for the story they tell.

Let's break it down in human terms.

1. Impressions: Are you being seen?

This is how many times your ad appeared in search results or on competitor pages.

Low impressions mean your keywords are too narrow or your bids are too low.

If you're invisible, even the best book in the world can't convert.

2. CTR (Click-Through Rate): Are you catching eyes?

CTR tells you how many people clicked after seeing your ad.

If your CTR is low, your cover or title isn't doing its job.

Think of it as your *digital handshake.* If no one's shaking your hand, it's time to freshen your presentation.

In the early stages of any campaign, aim for at least 0.10% CTR. That's your first proof of life... the sign that your cover and title are starting to grab attention. Once you cross that, keep testing visuals, bids, and copy until you steadily improve toward the 0.3%–0.5% range.

Those small percentage bumps add up fast. Higher CTR means cheaper clicks, stronger conversions, and clearer feedback about what resonates with your readers.

Remember, impressions are free until they're not... because if they don't turn into clicks, *Amazon* stops giving you more of them. High visibility without engagement isn't success; it's a warning sign.

3. CPC (Cost Per Click): Are you overpaying for attention?

This is how much you pay every time someone clicks.
High CPCs usually mean you're competing in a crowded niche… think "leadership," "self-help," or "real estate investing."
That's okay. Paying a little more for *quality* keywords is often worth it.

Just make sure you're tracking conversions, not chasing cheap clicks that never buy.

4. Conversion Rate: Is your listing doing its job?

This is where your Step 7 work gets tested. If people click your ad but don't buy, your problem isn't traffic; it's your listing.

Your title, cover, or description might not be convincing readers to take the next step.

Go back to *Step 7: Build a Launch-Ready Listing*.
Your ad might be doing its part by bringing people in, but your listing has to *close the deal.*

5. ACoS (Advertising Cost of Sales): Are you profitable?

This one scares authors because it looks like algebra.
Here's the simple version: ACoS tells you how much you spent to make each dollar in sales.

If your ACoS is 50%, that means you spent $0.50 to earn $1.00 in book sales.

Is that good or bad? It depends on your goal.

If you're in learning mode—building visibility, testing keywords, and gathering data—a high ACoS is perfectly fine.
Early campaigns aren't about profit; they're about insight.

As your ads and book listing improve, that number naturally drops.
Because the algorithm starts rewarding consistent conversions with lower costs and better placements.

The biggest mistake authors make is overreacting too soon.
They run ads for a week, don't see massive profits, and quit right before the data gets interesting.

But smart authors?
They treat those first few weeks or months like research and development.

They learn which keywords perform, which covers attract, and which price points convert.
Then they take that data, refine it, and start scaling what works.

Because every click tells a story... and your job is to listen long enough to hear the pattern.

Up next, we'll talk about how to do exactly that: how to *scale what works* and turn your data into growth.

Scaling What Works

Once your ads start running, it's tempting to stare at your dashboard like it's a stock ticker.

Sales up? You celebrate.
Sales down? You panic and hit pause.

But here's the truth: early Amazon ad campaigns aren't meant to make you rich; they're meant to make you *smart.*

The first few weeks (sometimes months) are about discovery, not profit.

It's like going to the gym for the first time... you're not there to win a fitness competition; you're there to figure out which muscles even exist.

During this phase, your ACoS (Advertising Cost of Sales) will often look scary.
100%, 200%, even 300%.
And that's perfectly normal.

Because at this stage, you're not buying profit; you're buying *data.*

Every click tells you something: which keywords attract interest, which covers get attention, and which phrases trigger conversions.
You're mapping the landscape.

Think of it as paying Amazon tuition.

You're investing in learning what actually works so that later, you can start scaling the winners and cutting the losers.

Here's the process:

- **Step 1: Identify your top performers.**
  Look for keywords with solid impressions, healthy CTR (0.3% or higher), and conversions.

These are your keepers. Move them into new manual campaigns where you control the budget and focus.

- **Step 2: Pause the money drains.**
  If a keyword is eating up spend with zero sales after a few hundred clicks, pause it.
  Don't get sentimental. It's data, not destiny.

- **Step 3: Recycle what you learn.**
  Take your best-performing keywords and weave them into your book's backend metadata, subtitle, and A+ Content.
  That extra relevancy boosts your *organic* discoverability... so *Amazon* starts showing your book more often without ads.

- **Step 4: Optimize your listing along the way.**
  If you're getting clicks but few sales, it's not your ad; it's your storefront.
  Tweak your title, refine your description, or adjust your pricing until your conversion rate improves.

  Every small optimization helps your ads perform better tomorrow than they did today.

- **Step 5: Scale gradually.**
  Once you find campaigns that consistently bring in sales at an acceptable ACoS (or even break even), start nudging your budget up.
  Small increases—10% to 20% at a time—build steady momentum without confusing the algorithm.

Remember: success with Amazon Ads is a compounding game.
The longer your ads run and the more you optimize your listing, the more efficient your campaigns become.

Eventually, your profitable keywords start pulling double duty... driving *paid* traffic and boosting *organic* rankings.

That's when you know the system is working *for* you, not against you.

So yes, you'll probably spend the first few weeks—or even a few months—in the red.
Don't panic. That's normal.

You're not losing money. You're investing in clarity.

Because the moment you know what converts, what doesn't, and what to scale, every dollar you spend stops being an expense and starts being an engine.

Up next, we'll explore how to build that momentum beyond ads—by using **organic traffic** to feed the algorithm just as effectively.

Organic Traffic That Feeds the Algorithm

Here's the part nobody tells you:
Not all visibility comes from ads.

Amazon Ads might be the engine that starts your momentum, but *organic traffic* is the wind that keeps it moving long after you stop paying for gas.

And the beauty of it? You already have the tools to make it happen.

Let's start with the most obvious one... *your link*.

When you share your book online, always send people to your Amazon listing, not your website.
Why? Because *Amazon* rewards you for every click and conversion that happens on its turf.

Every external visit that ends in a sale strengthens your book's credibility inside Amazon's system.
It's like saying, *"Hey, this book doesn't just sell when we promote it here; it sells everywhere."*

That's why one of the smartest moves you can make is to turn every platform you use—*LinkedIn*, *YouTube*, your email signature, podcast appearances, even that QR code on your business card—into a direct path to your Amazon page.

Not to a "learn more" page.
Not to a complicated funnel.
Just... Amazon.

Because again, *that's where the buying intent lives.*

There's one small—but smart—exception to this rule, which we'll get to later in this chapter. It's called the *Amazon Funnel*, and it's how you can ethically blend an email list strategy with Amazon's ecosystem without losing momentum or confusing the algorithm.

Now, a quick but crucial pro tip: *clean your Amazon link before sharing it.*

When you open your book's page, Amazon adds a mile-long trail of tracking code after the ASIN (the unique ID that looks like B09XYZ1234). You only need the clean part that ends right after the ASIN... like this:

https://www.amazon.com/dp/B09XYZ1234

Everything after that? Delete it.
Those extra parameters don't help you; they just make your links look messy and break easily when shared.

The Amazon Funnel Strategy

There's one smart exception to the "always send people straight to Amazon" rule... when you use a simple *Amazon Funnel*.

Here's how it works:
You create a short landing page that offers something valuable *only* to verified buyers.

Think along the lines of:

- A bonus chapter or short video training.

- A workbook, checklist, or companion guide tied to the book.

- Access to a private community or event replay.

Readers buy your book on *Amazon*, then upload their receipt or order number on your page to claim the bonus.

That one extra step does two powerful things:

1. It drives real sales on Amazon (feeding the algorithm).

2. It ethically captures your reader's email (building your ecosystem).

This is how you turn Amazon's traffic into *your* audience... without breaking their terms of service.

Just make sure the bonus feels like a genuine reward, not a trap.

Track What's Working

If you want to see which of your traffic sources actually perform, use *Amazon Attribution*.
It's a free tool that shows which external sources—like your newsletter, podcast interviews, or social media posts—actually drive sales.

You won't get personal buyer data (Amazon guards that like *Fort Knox*), but you'll get insight to refine your strategy.

Borrow Other People's Traffic

In Step 6, you learned how to seed monetization inside your book. Here, we're using those same outreach habits for a different goal: to feed Amazon's algorithm steady, high-quality traffic.

Your audience might be small, but other people's audiences aren't.
Every podcast guest spot, *LinkedIn* article, or webinar appearance is a traffic opportunity in disguise.

When you show up in someone else's ecosystem, you tap into trust that's already built.

That's organic visibility at its finest... borrowed credibility that compounds over time.

Each click, each post, and each mention adds another breadcrumb trail leading back to your Amazon listing.
And the more trails you create, the more the algorithm takes notice.

This is how you build lasting momentum without overspending.

Ads light the spark.
Organic traffic fans the flame.
And an *Amazon Funnel* captures the heat.

Together, they create the kind of sustained visibility that algorithms—and readers—can't ignore.

Up next, we'll see what happens when all those clicks and conversions start snowballing into something much bigger than visibility: *algorithmic momentum.*

The Snowball Effect

If you've ever tried to push a snowball uphill, you know how it feels to start marketing a book from zero.

At first, it's slow. Every click, every sale, every keyword tweak feels like a small push that barely moves the needle.
But stick with it long enough, and something magical happens.

Momentum.

Amazon's algorithm starts recognizing patterns:
People who search for your keywords tend to click your listing.
People who click tend to buy.
People who buy tend to leave decent reviews.

And suddenly, you're not pushing the snowball anymore.
It's rolling downhill... on its own.

That's when you start appearing in places you didn't even target:

- *Customers Also Bought* sections under bestsellers in your niche.

- *Recommended for You* carousels on shoppers' homepages.

- *Sponsored placements* you didn't even pay for (Amazon's "free samples" of organic visibility).

This is how consistent traffic—paid and organic—turns into algorithmic trust.

Because to *Amazon*, *trust* means performance.
If your book keeps converting, it's safe for them to keep showing it.

That's why consistency beats intensity.
It's better to run smart, steady ads for 90 days than to blow your budget for a week and disappear.

When your book's listing, keywords, and ads start firing in sync, the system begins to self-fund:

- Paid ads feed organic rankings.

- Organic sales lower your ACoS.

- Lower ACoS lets you scale ads profitably.

It's a flywheel... and once it spins, it gets easier to maintain and harder to stop.

By now, your Amazon Ads are gathering data and building steady sales. Let's look at another tool that complements them instead of competing with them.

BookBub: The Secret Partner in Visibility

Most authors think Amazon Ads are the only lever for traffic. But there's another quiet powerhouse... *BookBub Ads*.

BookBub's audience is made up of voracious readers... millions of people who buy eBooks daily.
If you're running digital editions, *BookBub* can often outperform Amazon Ads in cost per click and engagement.

Think of it like this:

- ***Amazon Ads*** are your main driver for visibility across all formats. They're especially powerful during your Kindle-first testing phase... helping you identify which keywords, titles, and covers convert. Once you roll out your print edition, those same ads keep fueling your rankings and physical sales.

- ***BookBub Ads*** specialize in eBook discovery... reaching passionate readers who love digital deals, series, and recommendations.

Used together, they're a one-two punch: Amazon Ads feed the algorithm with conversion data, while *BookBub* drives fresh discovery and low-cost clicks that amplify your reach.

Start small—just a few dollars a day—and measure which creatives and audiences perform best.
Then feed those insights back into your Amazon keyword strategy.

When *Amazon* and *BookBub* start "talking" through consistent sales signals, your snowball turns into an avalanche.

The algorithm takes over, traffic becomes self-sustaining, and your book keeps selling long after your last ad tweak.

That's the magic of momentum.

Remember, the goal isn't to chase quick wins; it's to teach Amazon's system who your readers really are and keep that signal strong.

The Myth of the One-Day Bestseller

Somewhere along the way, a strange myth took hold in publishing... that if you stack all your book sales on one magical day, you can "hack" the system, hit a #1 badge, and live happily ever after.

It sounds tempting, right?
Build a pre-order list, rally your friends, make everyone buy on the same day...
Watch your book skyrocket to #1 for a few glorious hours.

And then?

You fall off a cliff.

Amazon's algorithm isn't impressed by one-day miracles.
It's built to reward consistent, *sustained* performance—books that keep selling day after day.

When you dump all your sales into a single spike and then go silent, Amazon gets confused.
It thinks your book was a short-lived trend with no staying power.
And what does the algorithm do with spikes?
It buries them.

Even worse, many authors pair this "launch day hack" with another mistake: turning off ads right after launch.
That's like cutting the engine the moment your plane takes off.

The algorithm loses data, your sales velocity collapses, and your ranking begins its slow rollercoaster slide into obscurity.

Amazon doesn't reward intensity; it rewards *consistency.*

Steady traffic, reliable conversions, and gradual growth send a far stronger signal than a one-day sprint.

So instead of chasing a 24-hour bestseller badge, aim for a *90-day build*.
Let your ads run, keep traffic flowing, and train the algorithm to see your book as a long-term performer.

Because a short-term spike gets you a screenshot.
But consistent visibility gets you a career.

Momentum doesn't come from hacks; it comes from habit.
Keep feeding the algorithm with steady data, and it will keep feeding your visibility in return.

That's the loop that turns authors into brands.

Visibility Creates Velocity

By now, you've built the foundation, optimized your listing, and started driving intentional traffic.

Now the game shifts from *effort* to *momentum*.

Because visibility isn't just about being seen.

It's about *staying* seen.

Every click, every conversion, and every keyword that performs is another drop of fuel in your book's engine.

At first, you have to push it… test, tweak, reinvest.

But soon, the system starts helping you.

That's when the real fun begins.

The algorithm notices you.

Your ads self-optimize.

Your book starts showing up in places you never paid to be.

Suddenly, readers are discovering you on autopilot.

And what once felt like constant hustle starts to feel like gravity pulling your book into the spotlight.

That's the power of visibility-driven publishing.

You don't need a massive audience; you need traction.

You don't need luck; you need data.

You don't need viral moments; you need consistency.

Because once your book proves it converts, *Amazon* keeps feeding it to the right readers.

Visibility creates velocity.

And velocity compounds.

That's why smart authors play the long game, not the launch week.

They understand that what starts as paid visibility evolves into organic discoverability.

And that discoverability, over time, becomes credibility.

You've built it.

You've promoted it.

Now it's time to *leverage* it... turning your visibility into trust, authority, and proof.

You've mastered momentum; now it's time to turn that motion into meaning.

Up next... *Step 9: Turn Visibility Into Credibility.*

Because a bestseller isn't just a book that sells; it's a book that sells you.

Step 9: Turn Visibility Into Credibility

You're Famous for Five Minutes (Now What?)

YOU DID IT. YOU ran the ads, posted the videos, emailed your list, and watched the traffic roll in. For a moment, your book felt unstoppable. You refreshed your dashboard every five seconds. You took screenshots. You told your mom you were *"trending."*

Then... silence.

Because visibility isn't the finish line. It's the starting gun.
Getting noticed is easy. Staying trusted is the real challenge.

In a world where everyone is an *"Amazon Bestseller,"* being seen isn't enough. The real game isn't attention. It's belief.

Visibility gets attention. Credibility earns commitment.

The Proof Problem

Think about the last time you saw a viral video. You probably clicked, laughed, and forgot it existed by lunch.

That's visibility without proof... lots of eyeballs, zero belief.

Authors fall into the same trap. They chase reach, impressions, and ad dashboards like it's the stock market. But if people can't *verify* that you deliver what you promise, *Amazon* might show your book, but readers won't believe in it.

> *Here's the truth: people don't trust claims; they trust evidence. That's why social proof—reviews, testimonials, screenshots, blurbs—is the real currency of credibility online.*

On *Amazon*, verified reviews carry enormous weight. The number and freshness of verified reviews directly influence where your book appears in search results, and they tell both Amazon and readers that customers are happy with your product.

A book with ten verified reviews will outrank one with two. And a book that keeps earning new reviews will beat one that's been quiet for months.

Amazon's logic is simple: why show shoppers something no one seems excited about?

But the power of proof goes beyond algorithms... it shapes perception.

When a potential reader lands on your page, they're silently asking: *"Do I trust this author with my time, money, and reputation?"*

Every element on your page answers that question. The cover says, "I'm professional." The description says, "I understand you." The reviews say, "Others took the risk... and loved it."

Without that validation, even the best-written book feels like a stranger handing out business cards nobody asked for.

And here's the kicker: *credibility doesn't just build trust; it drives conversion.*

People rarely buy because they *saw* you; they buy because they *believe* you. Proof turns curiosity into commitment.

For new authors, this matters even more. When your book doesn't yet have reviews or ratings, readers look for *replacement proof*:

- A professional cover and description (signal competence)

- A strong author bio or credentials (signal authority)

- Endorsements or testimonials from others (signal trust)

- A well-optimized listing with clear benefits (signal reliability)

These early credibility cues tell readers, *"It's safe to take a chance on this one."*

Even before your first review lands, you can convert browsers into buyers—because they trust what they see.

Visibility gets you noticed. Proof earns the decision.

Reviews Are Proof, Not the Product

Before we go deeper, let's clarify something important.

Reviews don't create demand; they validate it.

Traffic brings people to your page. Reviews help them stay.

If you don't drive attention first, reviews won't save you. And if you drive attention without proof, conversion collapses.

That's why reviews live inside credibility, not visibility. They are not the engine. They are the evidence that the engine works.

Amazon Reviews: Your Public Reputation System

Why Reviews Matter

Every author wants five stars. Nobody wants to beg for them.

But let's be honest: reviews are one of the strongest trust signals in your book's long-term success.
They're not just about ego or bragging rights. They're about *trust*.

On Amazon, reviews serve two masters: the reader and the algorithm. The reader wants proof that the book delivers what it promises. The algorithm wants proof that people are buying, reading, and reacting.

When someone buys your book and leaves a verified review, Amazon treats it as a real signal: transaction and feedback combined. Because Amazon's goal is simple: *to sell what people love.*

Verified reviews directly impact your visibility, credibility, and sales momentum.

Publication Day Is Not Launch Day

Most authors treat publication as the moment to shout from the rooftops. That's backwards.

Publication is a technical event. It's when your book goes live and your listing stabilizes across formats. Whether digital or print, your goal is to ensure the page converts before you send traffic to it.

Nothing magical happens yet. And that's intentional.

During this quiet window, you:

- Confirm formatting

- Ensure your listing converts properly

- Allow early reviews to begin appearing

Then you amplify.

Sending traffic to a page with zero proof wastes momentum. Synchronizing proof before broad visibility increases conversion dramatically.

The Soft Launch Window

Early reviews matter most when they appear close together.
Not artificially. Not aggressively. But naturally within a short window that signals activity.

Amazon rewards patterns that look organic. Sudden spikes followed by silence raise eyebrows; steady activity builds trust.

Your goal is not to impress the algorithm.
It's to remove doubt for readers.

Launch Teams: Validators, Not Buyers

A launch team is not your market.
Their job is not to "make the book successful." Their job is to help establish early credibility while your book reaches strangers.

Small, aligned launch teams outperform large, disengaged ones.

Confusing applause with traction is how authors burn out after week one.

Reduce Friction: The Direct Review Link

Most readers who intend to leave a review never do.
Not because they didn't enjoy your book. Because Amazon doesn't make reviewing obvious.

The review button sits at the bottom of your listing. Many never scroll that far.

You can reduce friction by linking directly to the review submission page for your book. This takes readers straight to the star rating and review form.

This isn't gaming the system. It's respecting your reader's time.
Include it:

- At the end of your book

- In a post-purchase email

- In launch team communication

And if the link fails on certain devices, simply instruct readers to search for your book on Amazon and click "Write a review."

Remove friction. Don't pressure.

Verified Reviews, ARCs, and Free Promotions

Amazon prioritizes reviews tied to marketplace behavior.

Reviews from verified purchases carry more weight. Reviews from external files or early distribution sometimes appear lower or receive less visibility.

That doesn't mean ARCs are useless. It means timing and acquisition path matter.

Official free promotions inside Amazon can still generate verified reviews because Amazon records the transaction.

Free is not the problem.
Unaligned traffic is.

Review Momentum Takes Time

Reviews don't appear overnight.

Even if your launch goes well, it might be weeks or months before you see steady review activity. That's normal. It doesn't mean your book is failing; it just means your readers are human. They buy. They read. They get distracted by *Netflix*.

The secret isn't panic; it's *patience and process.*

You can (and should) remind readers to review your book, but it has to be done ethically and naturally:

- A short note at the end of your book thanking them for reading and inviting honest feedback.

- A gentle nudge in your post-purchase or follow-up emails.

- A QR code or link to make leaving a review easy.

No incentives. No manipulation. No "five-star for a gift card." Amazon can detect artificial enthusiasm quickly… and the penalty isn't worth it.

Consistency beats coercion.

Friends and Family: When Help Hurts

And here's another trap too many first-time authors fall into: *friends and family reviews.*

It's tempting, but those well-intentioned "support reviews" can hurt your book more than help it.

Here's why:

- Amazon's algorithm is smarter than you think. If your mom buys your business book but usually reads romance—or if your friends who normally purchase fiction leave reviews on your nonfiction title—the system gets confused. It starts recommending your book to the wrong audience, which can tank your conversion rate and hurt visibility.

- If multiple friends or relatives—or anyone directly connected to you—leave reviews, Amazon's filters may flag them as biased and remove them entirely.

- In repeat cases, Amazon can even restrict your book's advertising or review eligibility.

Amazon's review policy is built on reader authenticity, not relationships. It wants feedback from genuine buyers who fit your intended audience.

So, what should your friends and family do instead?
If they're genuinely interested in your book's topic and are part of your target audience, their purchase *and* review are fine. But if they're just trying to help out, ask them to buy the book, but skip the review. Their purchase still helps your ranking momentum while avoiding the risk of confusing the algorithm.

The goal isn't to collect praise.
It's to collect relevant proof from your actual audience.

The Danger of Over-Engineering Reviews

There's a point where review strategy becomes counterproductive.

Too many reminders.
Scripted templates.
Pressure tactics.

Low-quality generic reviews hurt more than they help.

Amazon favors authenticity. Readers sense exaggeration instantly.

A smaller number of specific, relevant reviews from your true audience outperforms inflated numbers every time.

Proof should feel earned, not manufactured.

Customer reviews are powerful because they come from the marketplace itself.
But they're not the only form of credibility you can leverage.

If you're new—or still waiting for organic reviews to build—you can borrow authority ethically and strategically.

Borrowed Credibility: Editorial Reviews, Media, and Awards

Here's the good news: even if you're new, you don't have to start from zero credibility.
You can borrow it… ethically and smartly.

Think of it like social borrowing, not financial. When someone credible vouches for you, their reputation rubs off on yours. It's the same reason we trust a restaurant featured in *Forbes* more than one with a handwritten flyer taped to a lamppost.

In the author world, that borrowed trust comes from three places: *editorial reviews*, *media mentions*, and *awards*. Together, they form your credibility trifecta.

Editorial Reviews: Bridging the Gap and Building Positioning

If you're launching a new book, there's often a credibility gap between publication day and the moment organic customer reviews begin to build.

That gap matters.

When readers land on your Amazon page and see little or no feedback, doubt creeps in. They're asking silently, *"Is this worth my time?"* Before your marketplace proof matures, you need credibility anchors.

That's where editorial reviews come in.

Editorial reviews are professional evaluations of your book from credible sources—industry experts, thought leaders, media outlets, or recognized review organizations. They are not customer opinions; they are third-party validations.

And they serve a different purpose.

Customer reviews signal marketplace response.
Editorial reviews signal professional endorsement.

Both matter. But editorial reviews give you something powerful early on: structured authority.

They appear inside your Amazon listing under the "Editorial Reviews" section and can also be featured in your A+ Content, author bio, website, and media kit. Used correctly, they do more than fill space. They frame perception.

An editorial review is not just feedback. It is positioning.

A strong quote from a respected expert or industry publication tells readers, *"This book has already been vetted."* That lowers friction. It reduces hesitation. It makes your message feel safer to trust.

The goal isn't quantity. It's quality.

A few specific, credible endorsements will outperform a dozen vague blurbs. Generic praise blends in. Targeted validation stands out.

Use editorial reviews intentionally:

- Feature your strongest excerpts inside the Amazon "Editorial Reviews" section.

- Add select quotes to your A+ Content or media kit.

- Include short endorsements in your website banner, LinkedIn headline, or email signature.

- Reference notable reviewers when pitching media or podcasts.

You're not just displaying reviews. You're curating evidence that your ideas matter.

And yes, you can source editorial reviews ethically through professional review services, independent reviewers, industry contacts, or your publisher's network. Just ensure they are authentic and clearly labeled as editorial.

Because when someone lands on your Amazon page, your reviews are your reputation. You can't control what readers will say—but you can control how quickly meaningful proof begins to show up.

Editorial reviews don't replace customer reviews. They bridge the gap until organic validation compounds.

And when positioned well, they don't just provide proof; they elevate your authority.

Media Mentions: Social Proof on Steroids

Next comes media coverage—interviews, podcast appearances, or even a simple feature on a reputable website.

Media mentions add two things:

1. *Validation.* Someone else thought your story was worth telling.

2. *Search equity.* When someone Googles your name, they see credibility, not obscurity.

You don't need a *New York Times* feature. A niche podcast or respected industry newsletter often delivers more relevant reach... and higher-quality leads.

The key is to collect and display your appearances strategically: snippets, logos, or quotes that reinforce your authority.

Just make sure they're real. (Spoiler: "As seen on my cousin's Facebook post" doesn't count.)

Podcast Guesting: Borrowed Trust at Scale

Most authors chase podcast size. Smart authors chase alignment.

Audience numbers are rarely visible and rarely predictive. What matters is whether the right people are listening.

A small, highly aligned audience can outperform a massive, distracted one. One listener in the right position can open more doors than thousands of passive downloads.

Podcast guesting isn't about reach; it's about borrowed trust.

When a host invites you on their show, they lend you credibility. Their audience already trusts them. Your job isn't to sell. It's to resonate.

Think in Momentum, Not Moments

Podcast guesting works best when you stop chasing immediate outcomes and start thinking in timelines.

Go into every appearance knowing:

- You may only truly reach a handful of people... and that's okay.

- One of those people may invite you to speak, feature you in a newsletter, recommend your book to a private group, or introduce you to another host.

- Momentum compounds quietly.

This mirrors the same principle behind reader seeding and long-tail book sales. You are placing ideas—and your authority—into the ecosystem. Not all returns are visible immediately. Some arrive months later.

This is why authors who quit podcasting after "no spike" never see results. They were measuring the wrong thing.

The Real Objective of Podcast Guesting

Selling books is a secondary outcome.

The primary objectives are:

- Authority positioning

- Relationship building

- Entry into adjacent ecosystems

- Discoverability beyond Amazon

Podcast guesting works when it is treated as **infrastructure**, not promotion.

If you don't enjoy conversations, storytelling, and sharing your thinking out loud, podcast guesting will drain you—and you won't stick with it long enough to matter.

Consistency beats intensity here.

Spiderwebbing Your Way Up

Most authors aim too high, too fast.

They pitch their "dream shows" first, get ignored, and assume podcasting doesn't work.

The smarter approach is *spiderwebbing*.

You start with:

- Smaller or less competitive shows

- Shows you're already connected to

- Hosts who share your values, not just your topic

You deliver a great interview.
You make the host look good.
You become a low-risk guest.

Then you move outward.

You look at:

- Who has already been on your dream shows

- Which of those guests you can realistically reach

- Which smaller shows those guests have appeared on

Each appearance builds social proof. Each conversation reduces risk for the next host.

Podcast producers are always looking for interesting people who *haven't* already been everywhere, but who are clearly vetted. Being introduced through the ecosystem makes you safer to book.

This is how authors without big brands end up on big shows.

Pitch Relevance, Not Your Book

Strong podcast pitches are not about your book.

They are about **why this conversation belongs in the host's world**.

The best pitches feel like the episode has already been produced. They:

- Fit the show's format

- Match the host's interests

- Serve the audience's current needs

Relevance is the bridge.

When you can clearly articulate why *this* message matters to *their* listeners—right now—bookings become easier and more consistent.

Timing Matters More Than Hustle

Podcast guesting works best when aligned with your launch timeline, but it does not end at launch.

Authors chasing bestseller lists will structure interviews differently than those focused on steady, long-term sales. Both are valid. The mistake is not choosing.

For long-term traction:

- Set a weekly goal for interviews going live

- Think in months, not days

- Continue post-launch without dropping off

Books don't stop selling after launch week. Neither should your visibility.

Handle Rejection Strategically

When a podcast says, *"Our schedule is full,"* that's not a dead end. It's feedback.

Strong authors respond by:

- Asking what topics resonate most with the audience

- Learning which episodes performed best

- Re-pitching with sharper relevance and timing

Rejection is often a signal, not a verdict.

Create Goodwill Before You Ask

Podcast hosts don't need more pitches.
They need appreciation.

Leaving a genuine review, referencing a specific episode, or acknowledging what you enjoyed about the show instantly sets you apart. Hosts always need reviews. Very few guests offer them.

Goodwill lowers resistance.

This matters even more if you're working with a booking agency. Agencies amplify what already works; they don't fix weak positioning.

Why Starting a Podcast Is Usually the Wrong Move

Many authors are told to start a podcast to promote their book.
This is almost always bad advice.

A podcast is a serious, long-term commitment. Starting one *just* to talk about your book creates something else you now have to market. Hosting a podcast alone does not sell books. You still need distribution.

Podcast guesting lets you borrow existing audiences without creating another platform to maintain.

If you have a bigger mission beyond your book, a podcast can make sense. Otherwise, it becomes friction disguised as strategy.

Why This Works Long After Launch

Podcast guesting compounds.

Episodes live forever. People discover them months or years later. Authority builds quietly. Introductions happen off-record. Opportunities surface indirectly.

This is not fast marketing.
It is durable positioning.

And for authors building authority—not just chasing rankings—it remains one of the highest-leverage promotion strategies available.

Awards: The Authority Accelerator

Finally, let's talk about awards… the ultimate credibility badge.

Nothing signals legitimacy faster than third-party recognition.

When your book is nominated, becomes a finalist, or wins, it tells the world: *this book matters.* Even a **nomination** is a credibility booster. It says your book has already stood out among hundreds of others and that publishing professionals saw something worth celebrating.

You don't have to wait until the results are announced to leverage it. Use *"Award-Nominated Author"* proudly from day one. It gives your Amazon listing, bio, and media kit an instant upgrade—a subtle cue that says, *"This book isn't just published; it's recognized."*

An award emblem or nomination badge on your cover, website, or Author Page doesn't just look good; it builds trust. It tells readers, *"You don't have to take my word for it—look who already did."*

Of course, not all awards are created equal. Some are marketing schemes with certificates and no real judging. But the right ones—those vetted and respected in the publishing world—can open powerful doors:

- Media interviews

- Speaking invitations

- Bulk-buy deals

- Foreign-rights opportunities

Smart authors don't chase vanity awards. They pursue credible, respected recognitions that genuinely elevate their positioning and open doors. Because every recognition you earn—nominated, finalist, or winner—multiplies your authority, and authority is the ultimate sales engine.

Show, Don't Tell

Here's the harsh truth: nobody believes experts who have to *say* they're experts.
But everyone believes the one who *shows* it.

That's the difference between shouting, *"I'm credible!"* and simply proving it through your work, your process, and your readers' results.

We live in a world that's allergic to empty claims. You can tell people how great your book is, or you can *show* them... through transformation, outcomes, and lived proof that it works. *Guess which one sells more copies?*

The same rule applies to your author brand.
Don't tell readers you're passionate; show them the nights you stayed up writing, the clients you helped, and the breakthroughs your ideas created. Don't tell them your method works; show the screenshots, testimonials, or data that prove it.

You don't need to fake "success." You just need to *document* it.

Sharing behind-the-scenes moments, real reader stories, and practical examples does more for your reputation than a dozen polished slogans ever could.

People don't connect with perfection; they connect with humanity.

Here are a few simple ways to *show* instead of *tell*:

- ***Share real transformations.*** Post a reader message, a review highlight, or a client success story tied to your book's promise.

- ***Show your process.*** Share behind-the-scenes clips, early drafts, or visual frameworks to reveal your journey.

- ***Highlight reader participation.*** Photos of people holding your book or quoting your ideas make your message tangible.

- ***Use screenshots and stats.*** Honest data points (like growth numbers or client results) add measurable credibility without bragging.

When you consistently share results and stories, something shifts.
Your readers start selling for you.

They become living case studies... not because you asked, but because they experienced what you taught and want others to know.

That's when visibility and credibility merge.
People stop seeing you as *another author* and start seeing you as *the* authority behind an idea that works.

Because credibility isn't a headline; it's a track record.

Platform Consistency

Imagine this: someone sees your book ad on *Amazon*, clicks your name, and lands on your *LinkedIn* profile.

Your book cover says "authority," but your profile picture looks like it was taken during the dinosaur age.

Your website hasn't been updated since your last birthday, and your "About" section still says, *"Coming soon."*

That's not credibility. It's inconsistency.

And confusion kills trust faster than a one-star review.

Readers don't just check your *book.* They check *you.*

They look for patterns—visuals, tone, and message—to decide whether you're the real deal or another "bestseller" who peaked on launch week and disappeared by Tuesday.

That's why *platform consistency* matters.

It's not about being fancy. It's about being *familiar.*

When your *Amazon Author Page*, website, and social platforms all look and sound aligned, it sends one clear signal: *This person is legit.*

Here's how to make that happen:

1. ***Keep Your Visuals Aligned***

    Your book cover, headshot, and brand colors should feel like they belong to the same narrative.

    If your Amazon Author Page presents a clean, professional image but your website feels visually inconsistent or overly chaotic, it creates friction. Readers won't know which version of you represents the real brand.

Consistency reduces doubt. Inconsistency raises it.

2. ***Sync Your Message***

Your author bio, tagline, and tone should tell the same story everywhere.

If your *Amazon* description promises transformation, your LinkedIn summary shouldn't sound like a résumé.

Keep it conversational, personal, and focused on the outcome your readers care about.

3. ***Showcase Your Proof Everywhere***

Those reviews, editorial quotes, and award nominations? Don't leave them buried on Amazon.

Feature them on your LinkedIn banner, website homepage, and even in your email signature.

Repetition isn't redundancy; it's reinforcement. Every time people see the same signals of trust, your credibility compounds.

4. ***Keep Activity Visible***

Silence online feels like a ghost town.

You don't need to post daily, but stay active: share an interview, repost a reader photo, or publish a quick takeaway from your book.

Visibility without life looks like an empty storefront.

5. ***Align the Look and Feel of Your Brand***

Readers notice details.

A polished website paired with a blurry *LinkedIn* banner says, "*I tried once.*"

A cohesive brand—clean visuals, clear fonts, and consistent imagery—says, "*I take this seriously.*"

Consistency compounds over time.
Each platform reinforces the next, creating a loop of trust that strengthens with every click.

When readers see the same message, tone, and authority across your ecosystem, they stop second-guessing and start believing.

That's the moment trust turns into momentum.

A consistent author platform doesn't just look professional; it feels trustworthy.
And when people trust you, they buy from you, recommend you, and remember you.

Proof Creates Profit

Visibility draws attention. Credibility builds belief. And belief drives action.

Your proof is more than reviews or awards. It's the consistency of your message, the strength of your positioning, and the evidence that your ideas work in the real world.

Ask yourself:

- *Does my online presence reinforce the authority my book represents?*

- *Am I demonstrating outcomes, not just making claims?*

- *Have I built a system that continually reinforces trust?*

Traffic can be bought.

Trust cannot.

When you stop chasing spikes and start building sustained proof, your book stops behaving like a product and starts operating like an asset.

And assets compound.

Step 10: Create Momentum Beyond Launch Day

The Post-Launch Hangover

It happens every time.

You hit *publish.* You pop the champagne. You post the obligatory photo of your book in your hands, grinning like you just won an Oscar. Your friends flood the comments with heart emojis and *"So proud of you!"*

For one glorious week, you feel like you've made it.

Then... silence.

Sales flatline. Your Amazon rank slides faster than a melting popsicle. Your inbox goes quiet... except for that one relative asking if you'll sign a copy "for exposure."

Welcome to the post-launch hangover.

Every author goes through it... the sobering moment when you realize the finish line you were sprinting toward was actually the starting line. Launch day isn't the victory lap; it's the warm-up lap.

Most authors make the same mistake. They treat launch week like a movie premiere—glitz, applause, and opening-night buzz—then walk off thinking the show's over. But the real wins come from running the full season.

But here's the truth: *books don't stay alive because of one perfect launch. They grow through consistent discoverability and reader engagement.*

Anyone can spike once. The pros stay visible forever.

If launch week is your wedding, the real work starts in the marriage—showing up day after day, keeping the spark alive, and feeding the relationship. The algorithm, your readers, and the market all reward one thing: movement.

Momentum isn't created by a single burst of glory. It's built through a rhythm of small, steady actions that keep your book alive long after the confetti's been swept away.

That's what this chapter is about... the art and discipline of staying visible.

The goal isn't to launch a book.
It's to build a book that keeps launching itself... every day.

The Myth of "*Set It and Forget It*"

There's a dangerous myth in publishing: *set it and forget it.*

You've probably heard it from a well-meaning author in a *Facebook* group: *"Once your book is out, the algorithm will take care of it!"*

That's like buying a treadmill and expecting it to burn calories while it's parked in the corner.

Books aren't static. They're living assets: little salespeople working for you 24/7 if you keep them fed.
The moment you stop giving your book attention, it stops giving you attention back.

Amazon's algorithm, for example, is like a toddler with a short attention span. It rewards movement: sales, reviews, traffic, and engagement. The moment you go quiet, it wanders off to the next shiny book in line.

That's why most launches fizzle. Authors think they've "done their part." They upload the book, run a few ads, get family to buy copies, and then wait for royalties to roll in.

But algorithms don't care about effort. They care about activity.

Just like in business. You don't go to the gym once and expect abs. You don't post one viral video and expect a loyal audience. You show up, you iterate, and you build momentum over time.

Treat your book like a marketing channel, not a one-time project.

That means checking your dashboard, tracking traffic, testing headlines, refreshing metadata, and making small updates that tell Amazon, *"Hey, this book's alive... keep showing it."*

Launch day was planting. Now comes watering, pruning, and fertilizing.

The authors who win long-term aren't the ones who wrote the best book; they're the ones who stayed in the game after everyone else went home.

Evergreen Visibility: Feed the Algorithm

Here's a secret most authors miss: *Amazon's algorithm has a short memory... it only remembers the books that keep showing up.*

If you stop feeding it, it forgets you exist.

That's why evergreen visibility matters more than launch-week fireworks. It's the quiet, consistent rhythm that keeps your book floating instead of sinking into the digital abyss.

You don't need to go viral. You just need to show life.

Small, steady signals remind Amazon that readers are still engaging. Stay active, and the system keeps your book in circulation.

Here's how to feed the machine without burning out:

1. ***Refresh Your Metadata and Keywords.***
   Amazon isn't a bookstore; it's a search engine that happens to sell books. Every few months, revisit your keywords and categories. Look at what's trending. Are new sub-niches emerging? Are other books ranking for phrases you never thought of?

   Swap in fresh, relevant keywords and update your book's backend metadata. Even a small tweak can reawaken the algorithm and introduce your book to new readers.

2. ***Keep Your A+ Content Fresh.***
Your A+ section is prime real estate: visuals, testimonials, and story snippets that make your book feel *professionally published.* Update it when you earn new editorial reviews or media mentions.

Think of it like redecorating your storefront window. You don't need a full makeover... one new quote or banner can make the display feel brand-new.

3. ***Run Ongoing Ads (Even Small Ones).***
Here's where most authors panic: *"But my ads aren't profitable yet!"*
That's okay. Ads aren't a slot machine; they're a data machine.

You're not trying to win every click; you're collecting feedback. Over time, you'll see which keywords convert and which audiences respond.

Yes, your ACoS (Advertising Cost of Sales) might look ugly for a while. That's normal. The early phase is about *learning,* not *earning.* Once you identify what works, you can scale with confidence.

And remember, a small daily budget beats a one-time blast every time. It's about staying visible—not gambling for quick wins.

4. ***Trigger Mini Ranking Bursts.***
Every few months, run a pricing promo or limited-time deal. This

reactivates your book in Amazon's ranking system and attracts a new wave of readers.

Pair the promo with a short email blast or a few social posts. The goal isn't to make money during the discount—it's to reintroduce your book to the algorithm. Think of it as giving your book a shot of espresso.

5. ***Keep Gathering Reviews.***
Reviews are social proof and oxygen for the algorithm. But remember: quality beats quantity. A single thoughtful review carries more weight than five one-liners.

Make it easy for readers to leave reviews—mention it gently in your follow-up emails or inside your reader magnet sequence.

And for the love of books, don't ask your mom's knitting group to write one.

The bottom line: evergreen visibility isn't about massive effort; it's about steady signals.

It's the author's version of compound interest. You don't see results instantly, but over time, the small, consistent actions stack up. Suddenly, that book that "slowed down after launch" becomes a quiet, steady earner that keeps ranking, converting, and reaching new readers month after month.

Momentum built through steady signals is powerful.
But sometimes steady isn't enough.

Sometimes your book doesn't need watering. It needs a spark.

Not a desperate blast. Not a gimmick. A controlled burst of energy designed to wake the algorithm up and remind the market you're still here.

That's where strategic acceleration comes in.

Free Promotions Are Accelerators, Not Strategies

At some point, every author asks the same question: *"Should I run a free promotion?"*
The honest answer is *only if you know exactly what you're accelerating.*

Free promotions are one of the most misunderstood tools in publishing. In the wrong context, they cheapen positioning, attract the wrong readers, and generate nothing but screenshots and temporary rank spikes. In the right context, they can restart algorithm movement, introduce your book to new audiences, and amplify an ecosystem that already works.

The difference is not the promotion site.
The difference is intent.

A free promotion is not a strategy. It is an accelerator.
And accelerators only work when there is something worth accelerating.

When Free Promotions Make Sense

Free promotions work best when they serve a clear role inside your visibility system:

- Restarting a stalled book

- Seeding Book 1 of a larger ecosystem

- Supporting a relaunch with improved positioning

- Driving exposure toward a defined CTA already embedded inside the book

If you cannot clearly define the purpose, do not run it.

Free does not create value. It removes friction.
And friction removal only works when value is already clear.

The Correct Sequence

If you decide a free promotion makes sense, use this order:

1. Decide your mechanism: Kindle Select free days or deliberate permafree.

2. Secure promotion site dates first.

Only after confirmation, lock the dates inside KDP.
Most authors do this backwards.
Amazon is the execution layer. Promotion planning comes first.

There are various platforms that distribute free or discounted ebooks, but the specific site matters far less than your positioning and timing. These platforms provide short-term exposure, not long-term audience building. They amplify what is already working.

Treat them as accelerators inside a system... never as the system itself.

What to Measure

Ignore downloads alone. Instead, track:

- Review velocity after the promo

- Post-promo paid sales

- Email signups or CTA engagement

- Downstream inquiries

If nothing moves beyond downloads, the promotion failed... regardless of rank.

A free promotion should create momentum you can capture, not noise you celebrate.

Repurpose Your Content

Here's the part most authors overlook: your book isn't a one-time performance; it's a content goldmine.

You already did the hardest part. You spent months (maybe years) distilling your best insights, stories, and frameworks into a single volume. That means you're sitting on an entire ecosystem of content... you just haven't sliced it yet.

Why write new stuff when you can remix what already works?

Think about musicians. When a song hits, they don't bury it after launch. They remix it. Perform it live. Drop an acoustic version. Collaborate on a duet. They milk that melody for all it's worth... and so should you.

Turn Your Book Into a Blog (or LinkedIn) Series

Each chapter can become its own standalone article or post.

Take one key idea—a case study, a quote, or a simple framework—and expand on it in 500–1,000 words. Add a hook, a story, and a takeaway. End with a soft mention of your book.

This builds SEO juice, keeps your message discoverable, and positions you as a thought leader, not a "one-book wonder."

Slice It for Social

The golden rule: one book = a hundred posts.

Pull punchy quotes, surprising stats, or "aha" moments from your chapters and turn them into short-form videos, carousels, or tweet threads.

- Record yourself reading one powerful paragraph... it becomes a 30-second Reel.

- Turn a key takeaway into a carousel titled *"3 Lessons I Wish I Knew Before I Wrote My Book."*

- Screenshot a testimonial and write a short post about how that reader's experience validates your message.

You're not reinventing content—you're repackaging wisdom.

Bring It to Life in Audio and Video

Podcasts, interviews, and live sessions are perfect for expanding your book's shelf life.

Pitch podcast hosts who serve your niche... or start your own mini-series discussing your book's biggest lessons. Readers love hearing the *behind-the-scenes* stories: what didn't make it into print, what you've learned since publishing, or what you'd tell your pre-author self.

It's not about selling the book; it's about keeping the conversation alive. And every time you share these moments, you're quietly inviting new readers in.

Bundle, Teach, and Cross-Pollinate

Once you've created posts, articles, and audio, bundle them into newsletters, webinars, or short courses.

Each one gives your audience another entry point into your message... and each path leads back to the book.

That's how you build awareness that compounds. Not through endless creation, but through strategic repetition.

Because here's the truth: most people haven't seen your best idea yet. And the ones who have probably forgot it by Tuesday.

Your job isn't to keep inventing; it's to keep reminding people why your message matters.

Collaborations and Partnerships

If you want your book to stay alive long after launch day, stop trying to do it alone.

The myth of the lone author—grinding in silence, doing everything themselves, fueled by caffeine and self-doubt—makes for a great movie montage. But in real life? It's a growth killer.

You're not Batman. You're an Avenger.

And Avengers don't fight alone.

Leverage Other People's Audiences (OPA)

Your book doesn't necessarily need new readers; it needs new *entry points*.

Reconnect with people who already serve your audience—podcasters, consultants, or fellow experts—and find ways to share each other's platforms so your audiences grow together.

Guest on their shows. Swap newsletter features. Co-host a free webinar. Offer each other's readers a bonus or bundle deal.

Think of it as audience cross-pollination: every collaboration adds fresh oxygen to your visibility fire.

And remember: you don't need A-list influencers. Micro-audiences are often better. A podcast with 500 loyal listeners who actually buy books beats one with 50,000 passive scrollers every time.

Bundle and Collaborate

Team up with other authors or creators for bundled offers.

If you wrote a book on leadership, pair up with a productivity expert or communication coach to create a "Lead Smarter" bundle—both books together for one special price.

You can also run joint giveaways or challenges that tie your books together by theme. It's fun, fresh, and keeps your book in circulation without feeling repetitive.

Turn Interviews Into Evergreen Traffic

Every podcast or guest appearance is a breadcrumb trail back to your book.

Ask hosts to include your book link in their show notes. Offer a free bonus or resource (like a checklist or downloadable guide) that ties into your book's content. Those small assets compound... turning every old interview into an ongoing traffic source.

Pro tip: create one short, catchy "guest bio" that clearly mentions your book's title and value in one line.

Example: "H.J. Chammas helps entrepreneurs publish books that build authority and revenue. His latest book, Publish, Promote, Monetize,

reveals the proven system behind hundreds of bestsellers."
Make it easy for others to promote you... and they will.

Collaborate with Your Readers

Partnerships don't have to be limited to influencers. Your readers can be powerful ambassadors, too.

Feature their success stories in your posts. Highlight a quote or testimonial they've shared about your book. Celebrate them publicly.

Every time you highlight a quote or testimonial, you create a ripple effect that readers love to see. Their network discovers your book organically.

Visibility multiplies through collaboration.

Your message might be yours, but your momentum depends on others.

Because in this game, solo is slow, but partnerships are exponential.

Corporate & Organizational Bulk Buys

Most authors think success means convincing one person at a time to buy their book.
That's the slowest possible way to grow.

There's a completely different game most authors never play, and it's one of the most powerful distribution levers available to non-fiction authors: *corporate and organizational bulk buying.*

When a leader decides a book matters, they don't suggest it.
They mandate it.

And when that happens, your book doesn't just get bought; it gets **read**.

In my previous life at Nestlé, our CEO mandated that everyone read *The Tipping Point*. Not recommended. Not optional. Required. Thousands of copies moved because one decision-maker believed the ideas inside that book mattered for how people thought, worked, and led.

That's the real power of bulk buys.
Not volume for vanity's sake, but *forced attention at scale*.

Why Corporate Bulk Buying Works So Well

Leaders buy books for three reasons:

1. *Alignment*
   The book reinforces how they want their people to think, behave, or decide.

2. *Efficiency*
   One book can communicate what dozens of meetings cannot.

3. *Authority Transfer*
   By choosing the book, the leader signals, *"This thinking matters."*

And here's the part most authors underestimate:

Even when a book isn't officially mandatory, people read what they believe will help them perform better or stand out. If leadership cares about a book, ambitious people will too.

That's why corporate bulk buying creates **real readership**, not just sales spikes.

This Only Works If Your Book Deserves to Be Read

There's an important warning here.

If your book is boring, bloated, or self-indulgent, bulk buying will backfire. I say this as someone who's been a *forced reader*.
When your boss assigns a book, you don't skim it; you suffer through it.

So if you want organizations to buy your book in bulk, it must be:

- Clear

- Useful

- Well-structured

- And, yes, **entertaining enough to respect the reader's time**

A mandated book still needs to earn its place.

How Corporate Bulk Buying Actually Happens

This is not about "hoping" companies discover your book. It's about designing for it.

The most successful authors approach this intentionally, often following a simple rollout:

Pre-Release (1–6 Months Before Launch)

- Identify industries, companies, teams, or associations that would genuinely benefit from your book

- Map decision-makers (CEOs, HR heads, L&D leaders, founders)

- Decide whether you'll offer discounted or complimentary copies

- Prepare a simple message explaining *why this book matters to their people*

Final Countdown (1–4 Weeks Before Launch)

- Finalize your outreach package (book + short letter + simple order option)

- Make it effortless to say yes

- Continue expanding your target list

Launch Week

- Send bulk order packages to selected organizations

- Focus on relevance, not volume

- One right organization can outperform a thousand random buyers

Post-Launch Momentum

- Follow up

- Refine messaging

- Use social proof as traction builds

- Rinse and repeat

This exact approach helped authors sell **thousands of copies early**, not through hype but through relevance and intentional distribution.

Why This Belongs in Your Promotion Strategy

Corporate bulk buying does three powerful things at once:

- Moves real volume

- Creates genuine readership

- Builds credibility faster than consumer sales alone

When teams, organizations, or institutions adopt your book, your authority compounds.

And unlike one-off launches, this creates a **repeatable promotion channel**.

The Bigger Idea

The goal is not to "sell books."
The goal is to embed your thinking inside systems, teams, and cultures.

That's how books stop being products and start becoming platforms.

And that's why corporate bulk buying isn't a nice-to-have tactic.
It's a serious leverage move for authors who want their ideas to actually live in the world.

Strategic Visibility: Expanding Beyond Your Platform

Up until now, we've been talking about visibility you can control.

Your content.
Your ads.
Your collaborations.
Your email list.
Your partnerships.

That's good. You should control what you can control.
But there's another level of momentum most authors never reach.

Visibility you do not own.

This is where authority compounds.

Because there's a difference between being visible inside your ecosystem...
and being visible inside the market's ecosystem.

One builds traffic. The other builds legitimacy.
And legitimacy is what opens doors.

Ads rent attention. Strategic visibility earns it.

PR Is Not Publicity

Let's clear something up before we go any further.

PR is not about getting your face on television.
It's not about collecting logos for your website.
And it's definitely not about posting "As Seen In" graphics every time someone mentions your name.

That's publicity.

Publicity chases attention.
Strategic visibility builds authority.

There's a massive difference.

Publicity says, *"Look at me."*
Strategic visibility says, *"This idea matters right now."*

Most authors pitch their book.
That's the first mistake.

Editors are not looking for books. They're looking for stories, angles, tension, and relevance.

Your book is not news.
That's not an insult. It's reality.

Media doesn't exist to promote products. It exists to serve audiences who are already paying attention to something.

So when an author sends an email that says: "I just wrote a book and would love to be featured..."

It goes straight into the digital graveyard.

Not because the book isn't good.
But because it isn't contextual.

The question is not, *"Is your book valuable?"*
The question is, *"Why does this matter right now?"*

That's the filter.

And once you understand that, everything changes.

Don't Pitch the Book. Position the Idea.

Think about why certain authors become media regulars.

Robert Kiyosaki didn't go on television saying, *"I wrote a personal finance book."*
He went on saying, *"Your house is not an asset."*

That sentence alone created friction.

It challenged what people believed.
It invited debate.
It demanded curiosity.

The book became the deeper explanation.

Mel Robbins didn't get invited on shows because she published a book.
She named a behavior people recognized in themselves: hesitation.

She gave it language.

She gave it a simple tool.
She made it usable in under a minute.

That's media gold.

Tim Ferriss didn't pitch productivity tips.
He questioned the 9-to-5 work model.
He reframed work itself.

The common thread?

> *They weren't promoting books.*
> *They were promoting perspectives.*

> *The book was the foundation.*
> *The idea was the headline.*

That's strategic visibility.

When you shift from *"How do I promote my book?"* to *"What belief does my book challenge?"* you stop chasing coverage and start creating relevance.

And relevance is what compounds.

Attach to Moments, Not Megaphones

Most authors think they need a bigger platform.
What they actually need is better timing.

Visibility expands when your message connects to something already happening.

A season.
A trend.
A cultural shift.
An industry tension.
A question people are already asking.

If your book is about leadership, tie it to performance review season or promotion cycles.

If your book is about productivity, September is not random. It's "back to work" energy.

If your book is about financial discipline, economic uncertainty isn't a threat. It's context.

You don't create attention.
You attach to it.

Editors think in segments, not in products.

Imagine a producer saying, *"Coming up after the break…"*

Which one sounds stronger?
"Author discusses their new book."
Or:
"Why most people are stuck in jobs they secretly hate… and what actually works instead."

Same author. Same insight. Completely different impact.

That's the "after the break" test.
If your idea doesn't pass that filter, it's not ready for amplification.

And here's the beautiful part.
You don't need a massive PR agency to begin practicing this.
You need relevance discipline.

Platforms like HARO and Qwoted exist for one reason: journalists publicly ask for expert commentary.

They don't ask, *"Who just launched a book?"*
They ask, *"Who can explain this?"*

When you respond to those requests, you train yourself to think like media.

You stop asking, *"How do I get featured?"*
You start asking, *"Where is my insight useful right now?"*

That shift alone upgrades your authority.
And authority—not exposure—is what creates momentum that lasts.

Keep the Conversation Alive

Here's the uncomfortable truth: silence makes readers forget you faster than a new release ever could.

After launch, most authors go quiet. They stop posting, stop emailing, and stop talking about their book altogether... as if mentioning it again might make them look desperate.

But nobody's thinking about your book as much as you are. You're not being repetitive; you're being consistent.

Momentum lives in conversation.

Stay in Touch With Your Readers

If you built an email list (and I really hope you did), use it.
Not to hard-sell, but to *share the journey.*

Talk about what you've learned since publishing. Share behind-the-scenes moments. Tell stories about readers who applied your lessons. Drop one actionable tip from your book each month and tie it to a real-world example.

People don't unsubscribe from authenticity. They unsubscribe from noise.

You're not bothering your audience; you're nurturing a relationship.

Create Mini Campaigns Around Seasons or Events

Your book doesn't have to stay static. Tie it to what's happening in the world.

If your book is about leadership, launch a "New Year Reset" campaign in January.
If it's about productivity, do a "Back to Work" push every September.
If it's about personal growth, connect it to International Women's Day, Mental Health Month, or any event that fits your message.

Relevance keeps you top of mind... and gives people a reason to rediscover your book.

Reward Engagement

Host reader challenges, Q&A sessions, or live discussions around a specific chapter or concept.

You don't need a fancy setup... just you, a webcam, and genuine curiosity.

Ask readers how they're applying your ideas. Celebrate their progress. When readers feel part of something bigger, they don't just buy a book; they join a movement.

And when they feel included, they share.

Keep Adding Value

Your book is the start of a conversation, not the end of one.

Keep giving people reasons to stay connected:

- Offer updated resources, templates, or bonus material that complements your book.

- Create a short video series expanding on one of your frameworks.

- Build a simple workbook or checklist based on your chapters.

- Share a free guide that summarizes your key lessons for new readers.

Each piece extends your book's lifespan and keeps your ecosystem active.

Momentum = Visibility + Conversation

If your book is out there but you're not talking about it, the algorithm isn't the problem... *silence is.*

The authors who thrive years after launch are the ones who keep showing up with stories, lessons, and updates.

> *When you keep the conversation alive, you remind the world*
> *that your message still matters.*
> *That's what turns a book from a product into a platform.*

Momentum Creates Legitimacy

There is something most authors misunderstand about bestseller lists.

They think you chase them.
You do not. You qualify for them.

Becoming a "bestseller" does not automatically mean people are reading your book. It does not mean your ideas are spreading. And it definitely does not mean you have built authority.

Today, it is still possible to manufacture a bestseller label through obscure categories, coordinated purchase spikes, or paid ranking packages. Some cost a few hundred dollars. Others cost tens of thousands.
They optimize for the badge, not the outcome.

Legitimate lists do not rely purely on raw sales numbers for a reason. Sales can be manipulated. That is why major lists look for broader validation such as distribution breadth, multi-format performance, media coverage, retail presence, public conversation, and signs of organic demand.

In other words, they look for momentum... and that is exactly what you have been building.

Here is the distinction most authors miss:

> *Being a bestseller is not the benefit of being a bestseller.*
> *The benefit is what you had to build to qualify.*

If you skip the work and buy the label, you miss the actual cake, not just the icing.

Now here is another layer most authors never consider:
Different bestseller lists signal different audiences.

Some skew toward business buyers.
Others toward mass-market nonfiction.
Others are toward lifestyle or personal development readers.

If your ideal reader does not pay attention to a particular list, landing on it may look impressive, but it will not move your business.

Audience alignment matters more than prestige.

We do not ask, *"How do we hit a list?"*
We ask, *"Where does our reader already pay attention?"*

There are situations where a bestseller label can be strategically useful, such as for stronger media positioning, higher speaking fees, or faster credibility in new markets. But in those cases, the list is a tactical amplifier inside a much larger system.

It is part of the strategy.
It is never the strategy.

We don't build hacks. We build systems...
Systems that generate conversation, attract partnerships, drive sustained visibility, and compound over time.

Sometimes those systems qualify an author for a list.
Sometimes they do not.

But every time, they build authority.
And authority is what monetizes.

From Bestseller to Legacy Brand

Your launch created a spark, but this is where you build the fire.

You've done what most never will: you finished the book, launched it, and made your mark. But now comes the real work... the part that separates the one-hit wonders from the enduring names.

Anyone can hit #1 for a day. The pros stay relevant for years.

That's because they treat visibility as a system, not a stunt.

They don't chase spikes; they build rhythm.

They know momentum isn't something you *get;* it's something you *build.*

Think of every small action you take—updating your keywords, posting a quote, running a low-budget ad, sending a thank-you email—as another log on the fire.

Each one might not look impressive on its own, but together, they keep the flame alive long after others burn out.

The authors who last understand this: a book doesn't end when it's published. It begins.

Consistency beats intensity.

You don't need to be loud; just present.

You don't need to go viral; just stay visible.

Because over time, presence turns into trust, and trust turns into brand.

That's the quiet power of momentum... *it compounds.*

Every touchpoint, every reader interaction, and every updated piece of content adds up to something bigger.

Your book stops being just a product on *Amazon* and becomes something far more valuable... a piece of intellectual real estate that earns attention, builds authority, and opens doors to everything that comes next.

A book that keeps selling.

A message that keeps spreading.

A brand that keeps growing.

This is what promotion actually looks like beyond launch week... not noise, not spikes, but sustained movement.

And that brings us to the next chapter.

Because once your visibility is working for you—once your credibility is built and your authority established—it's time to turn that attention into income.

Up next: how to monetize everything you've built, turning your book from a marketing asset into a business growth engine that pays you back many times over.

Your book isn't the finish line; it's the fuel for what comes next. Now it's time to turn that momentum into monetization.

Part III: Monetize
Don't Sell the Book; Sell What the Book Sells

LET'S BE HONEST. MOST authors secretly believe that once their book hits bestseller status, the money will start rolling in. They picture royalty payments showing up in their inbox, a few new clients knocking on their door, and maybe a friendly email from Jeff Bezos saying, "Nice job." But then reality shows up... and it's driving a Prius.

Because here's the truth: your book was never meant to be the business. It's the door *to* the business. You don't sell the book... you sell what the book sells.

Every author dreams of that magical moment when their book makes money while they sleep. And sure, royalties are nice. They buy you an espresso or two. But the real money—the kind that changes your business and your impact—doesn't come from the book. It comes through it.

Think of your book like a movie ticket. The ticket doesn't make *Hollywood* rich; the franchise does. The ticket gets you in the door. The popcorn, the merchandise, the sequels, the theme park rides... that's where the profit lives. Your book works the same way. It's the ticket that gets readers inside your world... where the real value begins.

In the last part of this journey, you learned how to create visibility and credibility. You built momentum. You got people to notice you, trust you, and engage with your message. But visibility alone doesn't build a business. It's not enough to be seen—you need a way to turn that attention into income.

Your book gives you credibility, but what you build around it gives you consistency. The book is the handshake; your ecosystem is the partnership. It's what moves readers from *inspired* to *involved...* from people who love your message to people who live it with you. Without that next step, readers finish your book, close the last page, and vanish back into the internet.

Most authors stop there. They treat their book like a souvenir instead of a system. But the most successful ones see their book as the front door: a trust bridge that leads readers into something bigger. Every page, every story, every insight becomes a breadcrumb leading readers toward transformation. That's where the real value lives—in the ecosystem your book opens up.

Your book isn't the prize. It's the proof. It doesn't just share ideas—it builds belief. It doesn't just inform—it connects. And that's the real shift: from being an author to becoming an authority.

When I say your book is a system, not a souvenir, I'm not speaking in theory. I've lived it. Twice. The first time was back in 2007, when I read *Rich Dad Poor Dad.* That book completely changed how I thought about money. It told me what to do—build assets, think differently about wealth—but it never told me how. And that was the genius of it. The book wasn't the product; it was the gateway. It built enough trust for me to explore Robert Kiyosaki's courses and programs. That's where the transformation—and the real business—happened.

Years later, a different kind of book changed my personal life. It was called *A Man's Guide on How to Save Your Marriage Without Having to Talk About It.* That book helped me understand myself and my relationship more deeply. But more importantly, it built trust. That trust led me to the author's coaching program, which truly transformed my life.

Two very different books. Two identical lessons. A book doesn't just sell ideas; it sells belief. And belief opens doors: to change, to business, to something bigger.

Now that you've built your foundation and earned attention, it's time to connect the dots. In this final part of *Publish, Promote, Monetize,* we'll turn your book into a living, breathing business engine... one that grows your income, your audience, and your impact long after launch week is over.

Here's what's ahead.
In Step 11, you'll build your author ecosystem—the foundation that connects your readers, your message, and your offers so no one falls through the cracks.
In Step 12, you'll design offers that scale your impact—transforming your expertise into programs and services that expand your reach
In Step 13, you'll fuel the system with smart traffic, bringing the right people into your world through meaningful, consistent visibility.
And in Step 14, you'll learn how to systemize it all, so your book keeps working for you long after you've moved on to your next big idea.

You've built trust. You've built traction. Now, it's time to make it profitable.

Step 11: Build Your Author Ecosystem

You Built a Bridge to Nowhere

MOST AUTHORS DON'T FAIL because they wrote a bad book. They fail because they didn't know what to do *after* it.

They spend months polishing every sentence, upload to *Amazon*, hit "publish," and wait for the magic to happen.

Sales trickle in. A few reviews appear. Someone even messages them on *LinkedIn* saying, *"Your book really inspired me!"*

And then... silence.

That reader—who could have become a coaching client, a course student, or even a lifelong fan—just disappears into the *Amazon* abyss. No connection. No follow-up. No next step.

Congratulations. You built a bridge to nowhere.

Here's the truth nobody tells you: *your book isn't a business. It's an entry point.*

A great book is a *trust pathway*. It carries people from curiosity to connection. But if your system doesn't lead anywhere—no website, no lead magnet, no structure—it's like inviting guests to your home and forgetting to build the front door.

Every author dreams of impact, but impact without infrastructure is just applause that fades into silence.

Your readers want more. They just don't know where to go next.

And that's where your ecosystem comes in.

The Ecosystem Mindset

Let's get one thing straight: *your book is not your business.*
It's the front door... the invitation. The friendly handshake that says, *"Hey, come on in. Let me show you something that can actually help."*

Without an ecosystem, readers come and go like tourists. They visit once, take a quick selfie with your book, and move on to the next destination.

But with an ecosystem, you give them a reason to stay... and a path to grow with you.

Think of it like this: your *book* builds awareness, but your *ecosystem* builds relationships.

And relationships are where the real ROI lives.

An ecosystem connects all the dots—your website, your email list, your lead magnets, your offers, your social content, even your *Amazon* page—into one living, breathing system that turns readers into lifelong fans (and often, paying clients).

When you get it right, your book becomes the entry ticket to a much bigger experience.

A reader finishes your chapter, lands on your website, downloads your free guide, joins your email list, and gets a helpful follow-up that deepens the relationship.

From there, they take the next step... maybe signing up for your course, attending your workshop, or booking a consultation.

All because you built a simple, connected path for them to follow.

Imagine if every reader who loved your book knew exactly what to do next, without you lifting a finger.

That's what an author ecosystem does: it automates connection and turns curiosity into conversion, day and night.

And here's where *hybrid publishing* quietly becomes your hidden advantage.

Traditional publishing locks your links, owns your data, and limits how readers can interact with you. But when you own your publishing rights, you control your ecosystem. You decide what readers see next, where they go, and how they journey deeper into your world.

That's the power most authors never tap into.

Because the goal isn't to *sell a book;* it's to *build a bridge.*

And that bridge starts with a few simple, connected parts.

The Core Components of an Author Ecosystem

If your book is the *hello,* your ecosystem is the conversation that follows.

It's what takes a reader from *"I liked your book"* to *"I can't stop following your work... where do I sign up?"*

Here's what that looks like in practice, without the tech overwhelm or the 47 moving parts you'll never use.

1. Your Website: Your Home Base, Not a Storage Unit

Your website isn't an online résumé. It's your *home base:* the one place where readers can land, explore, and feel like they belong in your world.

Too many authors treat their websites like digital junk drawers: a photo here, a random "About" paragraph there, and maybe a lonely "Contact" page emptier than a fridge at midnight.

You don't need a 10-page website. You need one clear path.

One page that tells visitors three things immediately:

1. *Who you help*

2. *What problem you solve*

3. *What to do next*

If your site doesn't answer those questions within five seconds, you're losing attention faster than a short-form video scroll.

Think of your website as your author hub: the single destination where everything connects.

It's where your book lives, your lead magnet sits, and your offers are visible and accessible. Everything else is optional.

And remember, simple always converts better than complicated.

2. Lead Magnets: Your "Let's Keep in Touch" Button

Once a reader lands on your site, the next question they ask (silently) is, *"What now?"*

If you don't give them something to do, they'll do nothing.

That's where your lead magnet comes in.

A lead magnet is your "let's keep in touch" button... something valuable enough that readers happily exchange their email for it.

It could be:

- A one-page checklist that complements your book

- A short video expanding on a key chapter

- A quiz that helps readers self-assess where they are

- A bonus chapter, worksheet, or behind-the-scenes story

You're not bribing them; you're serving them. You're giving them a reason to keep learning from you without having to buy another book.

And here's the secret: it doesn't have to be big. The smaller and more specific, the better.

If your book helps people start a business, your lead magnet might be *"7 Questions to Validate Your Idea."*
If your book is about productivity, it might be *"The 10-Minute Morning Reset."*

One promise. One quick win. That's all it takes.

3. CRM + Email Nurture: Your Invisible Assistant

Now that you've captured attention, what happens next?

This is where your CRM—your invisible assistant—steps in.

It never sleeps, never forgets, and never fails to follow up.

When someone downloads your lead magnet, your CRM automatically sends them a warm welcome email, thanks them for joining, and keeps the conversation going.

But here's the golden rule: *automation doesn't mean robotic.*

Write your emails like you're talking to one person, not an audience.

One story. One insight. One moment of real value.

Your goal isn't to impress; it's to connect.

Share stories, lessons, and personal insights that expand on your book's message. Remind readers why they trusted you in the first place.

That's how you turn fans into clients... through small, consistent, meaningful touchpoints.

Automation builds relationships at scale.
Authenticity keeps them for life.

4. Call-to-Action Pathways: Design the Reader's Journey

If your website is the home and your emails are the conversation, your call-to-action pathways are the roadmaps that guide readers through your world.

Most authors don't have a map. They have a maze.

They tell readers, *"Go to my website... or my LinkedIn... or maybe check out my YouTube."*

Confused readers don't buy; they bounce.

You need one clear path that answers the reader's biggest question: *"If I loved this book, what should I do next?"*

For example:

- A reader finishes Chapter 5, where you teach about building a brand.

- Your follow-up email shares a short video expanding on that lesson.

- At the end of that video, you invite them to book a free "Brand Clarity Session."

That's a simple, natural flow... no pressure, just guidance.

When you design your ecosystem this way, every chapter becomes a gateway, every interaction a relationship builder, and every email a step toward your offers.

Common Mistakes That Kill Momentum

Most authors try to build an ecosystem and end up tangled in one instead.

They follow fifteen different "guru" playbooks that all promise *"the ultimate funnel."* Before long, they're juggling five tools, two landing pages, and one big headache.

Here's where things usually go wrong.

1. Sending Readers to a Generic Website

Picture this: a reader finishes your book, inspired and ready to take action. They click the link on your "About the Author" page and land on your homepage.

What do they see?

A smiling headshot, a third-person bio, and a few random menu tabs.

Momentum killer.

If someone just spent hours with your voice in their head, don't send them to a generic corporate page. Send them somewhere that continues the conversation... a landing page made *just* for readers of your book.

Something like, *"Thanks for reading! Here's your bonus training,"* or *"Download your companion workbook here."*

Your book audience isn't cold traffic. Treat them differently.

2. Using Ten Different Tools That Don't Talk to Each Other

We've all been there. One platform for email. Another for landing pages. A third for payments. A fourth for scheduling.

And none of them sync.

So instead of running your business, you're running customer support for your own system.

Every time you add another tool, your ecosystem loses a little oxygen.

Keep it lean: one reliable CRM, one landing page builder, one calendar, and one email tool. That's enough.

You don't need tech superpowers; you need simplicity.

3. Failing to Track What Happens After the Click

Let's say your book link gets 500 clicks. Great.

But do you know what happens next?

Most authors don't. They have no idea who's signing up, what page performs best, or which call-to-action converts.

If you don't track, you can't improve.

You're not guessing whether your book is reaching people; you're measuring how deeply it connects.

Use simple tracking tools: Google Analytics, UTM links, or your email platform's own reports. You don't need dashboards that look like NASA's control room; you just need to know what's working.

Numbers don't tell the whole story, but they show you where the story's strong.

4. Overcomplicating the Funnel Before Validating It

This one quietly kills creativity.

Too many authors spend months designing complex funnels before they've validated their core message.

They create twelve-step email sequences, hire expensive designers, and write forty follow-ups... only to realize they built the wrong thing beautifully.

Don't build a mansion before testing the tent.

Start small. Launch one page. Offer one simple lead magnet. Send a short email sequence to a small audience.

Once it works, *then* scale it.

Because the best ecosystems don't start big; they grow big because they work.

Keep It Simple, Keep It Connected

Here's a secret most marketing experts won't tell you: your author ecosystem doesn't need to be fancy. It just needs to work.

You don't need animated buttons, seven landing pages, or a funnel map that looks like a NASA launch sequence.

You need one clear path.

One book. One lead magnet. One nurture sequence. One offer.

That's it.

When everything connects, magic happens.

A reader finds your book on *Amazon*.
They scan the first few pages and see a short link: *"Grab your free bonus guide at [YourWebsite].com."*
They visit your page, drop their email, and get an instant thank-you note from you.
A few days later, they open an email where you share a quick story, a small win, and an invitation to go deeper—maybe join your course, book a call, or attend your workshop.

All of that happens automatically.

That's the power of an ecosystem. It doesn't shout; it speaks consistently.

It doesn't chase readers; it attracts them.

And it doesn't rely on luck or algorithms; it relies on a system that turns every reader into an ongoing relationship.

Think of it like this: your *book* sparks interest, your *ecosystem* fuels it, and your *offers* keep it alive.

Most authors stop after that first spark. They publish, celebrate, and then wonder why the fire goes out.

Because they never built anything to keep it alive.

Don't build a spaceship when a bicycle will get you there.

Start small. Get one thing working. Then connect the next piece.

That's how you build momentum that never stops.

And once your ecosystem is flowing, when every part works together and readers have a place to go next, that's when the real fun begins.

Because now, it's time to fill that ecosystem with offers that multiply your impact and income without multiplying your workload.

Your Book Was Never Meant to End

When you really think about it, your book isn't a conclusion. It's a beginning.

Every reader who reaches the final page is silently asking one question: *What's next?*

If you don't answer that question, *Amazon* will. It will recommend another author's book, another story, another voice.

But when you build an ecosystem, you keep the conversation going.

You turn a single transaction into an ongoing relationship.

That's how impact compounds... not from one-time sales, but from continuous connection.

And here's the best part: *ecosystems don't just serve you; they serve your readers. They give them direction, momentum, and the next step to keep growing through your world.*

Your book opens the door. Your ecosystem keeps it open.

Once that foundation is in place—your website, your lead magnet, your email nurture—you've built the runway.

Now it's time to put something on that runway that actually takes off.

Because while your ecosystem keeps readers close, your offers are what move them forward.

In the next chapter, we'll design those offers: the scalable, sustainable ways to multiply your impact and income without multiplying your workload.

Monetization begins with connection and thrives on trust.

Step 12: Design Offers That Scale Your Impact

When Authors Confuse Impact With Busyness

In Step 11, you built the system that keeps your message moving... your *author ecosystem*. Now it's time to put that system to work by designing offers that turn connection into transformation... and transformation into income.

Let's be honest... some authors treat *impact* like a gym membership. They sign up for everything, sprint hard for two weeks, then collapse, wondering why they're exhausted and broke.

You've probably met the type. They're doing all the things: one-on-one coaching, free webinars, podcasts, online courses, and every event that offers a microphone and a lukewarm coffee.

Their calendar looks impressive... packed with meetings and Zoom calls that sound important. But their bank account? Not so much.

They confuse movement with momentum.

I know because I've been there. Early in my author journey, I thought success meant saying *yes* to every opportunity that "could" lead somewhere. Coaching sessions, interviews, masterminds, random summits with five attendees and one distracted host... I did them all.

One day, I proudly told a friend, "I'm booked solid this week!"
He smiled and asked, "Cool. For what?"

That question hit harder than a caffeine crash. I wasn't building a business; I was building burnout.

Most authors fall into this trap because they equate *serving more people* with *doing more work.* It feels noble. It feels like impact. But it's really just trading one job (your day job) for another (your book business)... except now you've got no weekends, no boundaries, and no boss to blame.

> *Real impact doesn't come from doing everything yourself.*
> *It comes from designing offers that multiply your value without*
> *multiplying your hours.*

You don't need more products.
You need smarter pathways.

From "Time-for-Money" to Scalable Value

Imagine your book becomes a hit. Readers start reaching out, saying things like, *"Your story changed my life!"* or *"Can I hire you for coaching?"*

Of course, you say *yes*... you love helping people.

Fast-forward three months. You're on your fifth back-to-back Zoom call, explaining the same concept for the tenth time, and wondering if you should've just written a book about stress management instead.

That's when it hits you: you didn't build freedom; you built a calendar prison.

Most authors accidentally create businesses that depend on them being in the room for every dollar earned. It feels productive at first, but it's really *time-for-money 2.0...* the author's version of a treadmill. Lots of motion, zero progress.

The shift that separates busy authors from profitable ones is realizing your biggest asset isn't your *time;* it's your *transformation.*

The ideas, frameworks, and insights you share are repeatable. They can be packaged, recorded, or supported by systems and teams that keep working long after the first conversation ends.

Because scaling doesn't mean removing yourself; it means showing up *where you matter most.*

At *Authority Publishing,* for example, every author still starts with a call with me. That conversation is crucial. It's where I listen, understand, and help them see what's possible. But once that vision is clear, my team takes over... editors, designers, and marketing specialists who turn the plan into results.

That's scalable value: showing up for the connection, not the repetition.

When your book introduces someone to your world, the next logical step *should* be to connect... so you can guide them into a system that delivers results through your frameworks, your processes, and your team.

That's how you scale *authentically...* one personal call at a time, powered by systems that do the rest.

The Three Scalable Offer Models

Let's clear up a myth right away: *scaling your impact doesn't mean disappearing from your business.*

It means showing up *where you matter most...* and designing systems, content, and teams that keep delivering your transformation long after that first conversation.

Think of it like conducting an orchestra. You still lead the symphony, but you don't need to play every instrument.

That's the beauty of scalable value: you remain present at the moments that matter most, while your systems, frameworks, and people help carry your message forward.

You've built the foundation... now let's turn it into scalable action. Here are three proven models that expand your reach, revenue, and impact without stretching you thin.

1. Coaching to Courses

If you're already doing one-on-one coaching or consulting, congratulations... you've proven people will pay for your transformation. But that also means your growth is limited by your calendar.

The key isn't to remove yourself. It's to replicate your best moments—the lessons, tools, and breakthroughs—and turn them into group programs or digital courses.

That way, you're still the *face* of the transformation, but the delivery happens through structure and systems that scale.

> *You record once. Your message keeps working.*
> *You guide the journey. Your systems handle the heavy lifting.*

You're not scaling *away* from you; you're scaling *through* you.

2. Speaking to Systems

If you're a speaker, you already know the rush of inspiring a room full of people. But here's the problem with applause... it doesn't scale.

The moment ends, the impact fades, and you're on another flight doing it all again.

The solution? Turn your signature talk into a repeatable system... a workshop, a course, or even a licensed training package that organizations can deliver without you having to be in the room.

> *You still own the IP. You still set the direction.*
> *But now your message works in rooms you'll never have to fly to.*

That's how you move from performing to multiplying.

3. Consulting to Communities

If you're a consultant, your clients love your insights... but it also keeps you on the clock.

The scalable version is to build a *membership, mastermind,* or *community* model where your clients and readers can access your frameworks, tools, and network... guided by your team and supported by each other.

You still show up for the high-level strategy sessions and "hot seat" moments, but the day-to-day engagement happens inside the community.

That's how you stay central to the value without being swallowed by it.

Scaling isn't about replacing yourself. It's about *amplifying* yourself.

Your readers don't want a clone of you; they want continued access to your thinking, your process, and your presence.
And that can happen through programs, platforms, and people you've trained to extend your impact.

Your book introduced them to your world.
Your scalable offers keep them living in it.

These models are your tools for scale. Now, let's organize them into a simple, logical journey... your *Value Ladder.*

Designing Your Value Ladder

In Step 6, we built the *pathways* inside your book... those soft bridges that turn readers into relationships. Now, Step 12 decides what those bridges lead to: the offers that deliver your transformation at scale.

Back then, we talked about the *Monetization Pyramid*: how to plant the seeds of income right inside your book. This time, we're moving up a level: designing the full *Value Ladder* that turns those early seeds into a self-sustaining business model.

Not every reader is ready for the same level of commitment. Some want to dip a toe in, others want the guided tour, and a few want the VIP experience. That's what your Value Ladder organizes... clear steps that match where each reader is in their journey with you.

Imagine walking into an *Apple Store* and seeing just one product on display... a single iPhone under a spotlight with a sign that says, *"Take it or leave it."*

That's how most authors design their businesses.

They have one offer—maybe a coaching program, a course, or a consulting package—and then wonder why sales feel like pushing a boulder uphill.

The truth is, not everyone who reads your book is ready for your premium offer. Some want to dip their toes in before diving into the deep end. Others are already convinced and just want the VIP experience.

That's where your *Value Ladder* comes in.

It's the simple idea that readers need different levels of engagement... and you should meet them wherever they are in their journey with you.

The Free Step: The Book

Your book is the front door to your world. It's free in spirit... readers might pay $15 or $22 for it, but what they're really buying is *trust.*

This is your handshake moment. The first impression that earns you permission to show them what else you can do.

The Low Step: The Entry Offer

Once readers love your book, they're asking a silent question: *"Okay, what's next?"*

Give them a low-friction way to keep learning... something that requires little commitment but delivers a quick, tangible win.

That could be a mini-course, a short workshop, a report, or a simple workbook that helps them take the first practical step from your book's promise.

Think of this as your *stadium seat.* Not everyone can afford front-row access, but they can still join the game.

The Mid Step: The Core Program

This is your signature transformation... the main system, coaching framework, or consulting process that takes clients from *Point A to Point B.*

If your book is the map, this is the guided tour.

At this level, you're not just giving information; you're leading implementation. It's where your expertise turns into measurable results.

The Top Step: The Premium Experience

Finally, for the readers who want your full attention—the ones who say, *"I want you, not just your method"*—create a premium tier.

This could be a mastermind, private consulting, or a done-for-you solution delivered by your team under your direction (like we do at *Authority Publishing*).

It's the top rung of the ladder... fewer clients, higher investment, deeper partnership.

The beauty of the *Value Ladder* is that it creates *momentum by design*.

Each step naturally leads to the next. No cold selling. No awkward pitches. Just a smooth journey where readers keep moving deeper into your world... at their own pace, guided by their own readiness.

Your goal isn't to trap them. It's to *guide them.*

> *Every offer you create should serve one purpose: helping readers go further in the transformation your book began.*

How to Price Without Panic

Pricing your offers feels a bit like standing on a diving board... you know the water will probably be fine, but your brain still whispers, *"What if it's freezing?"*

Every author hits that moment... the awkward pause between *"I've created something valuable"* and *"But who am I to charge that much?"*

Here's the truth: *if your pricing doesn't make you at least a little uncomfortable, you're probably undercharging.*

Price the Transformation, Not the Time

People don't buy based on how many hours you'll spend with them. They buy based on the *transformation* you deliver.

That's why charging for your time quietly caps your income. It ties your worth to your calendar instead of your contribution.

When you price based on transformation, you start valuing your results instead of your hours.

If your offer helps someone generate $10,000, save six months of frustration, or land their dream role, charging $2,000 isn't expensive; it's logical.

And remember: *clients aren't paying for how long it takes you. They're paying for how long it took you to learn how to do it that fast.*

The Psychology of Price

I once ran a workshop for $97 that people loved. A year later, I delivered the same workshop for $997... and people thanked me *more*.

The content didn't change. Their *perception* did.

Low prices attract dabblers. Higher prices attract doers.

When people pay more, they show up differently. The investment creates commitment.

So instead of lowering your price to make people feel safe, raise your value so they feel confident.

Lessons from the Field

Earlier, we looked at how a strong ecosystem turns visibility into credibility. Now, let's talk about what happens when you put the right *offer* and *pricing* behind that credibility.

When we first started, we made the same mistake most authors and coaches make: we priced for comfort, not for impact.

Take Paulette, an HR consultant who came to us after publishing her book on accountability with another company. She'd spent a fortune, launched with high hopes... and sold almost nothing.

We republished her book, repositioned her message, and aligned every-thing—from the cover to the categories—with what her *real* audience wanted. Within two months, it became a bestseller, but more importantly, she learned how a properly positioned offer could multiply her book's impact.

But here's the twist: the book didn't just sell copies; it opened doors. Corporate clients began booking her for workshops and training programs

worth around $50,000 in the first six weeks.
Project that across a year, and that's nearly half a million dollars in new business... born from one book.

And yet, when we looked back at what we'd charged, it was a fraction of that... maybe less than three percent.
That's when it clicked: we were pricing our *effort*, not our *impact*.

That's the same mistake most experts make. They charge for the work, not for the worth.

Where Paulett's story shows how pricing confidence amplifies results, Melkart's shows how niching down and packaging expertise create exponential scale.

Melkart wrote a book about customer service... a crowded topic if there ever was one. But he found his niche: the five-star hotel industry.

Through his book, HR directors and training managers from luxury hotels started calling him to train their teams. His book became his credibility badge... a golden key that unlocked a seven-figure training business.

Even if the project had cost $100,000 to create, it still would've been a tenth of what his book produced.
That's the *10× Rule* in action: if your client's outcome is ten times greater than their investment, everyone wins.

This isn't about publishing success; it's about system success... taking one idea and multiplying it through repeatable delivery.

Some authors scale through products. Others, like Sadika, scale through positioning... by transforming one clear message into consistent paid opportunities.

Sadika came to us with a powerful manuscript on women's empowerment that lacked focus. We helped her reshape it into a clear nonfiction book on gender balance and leadership... aimed at corporate audiences in the Middle East and Southeast Asia.

The result? Immediate traction.

She became a two-time TEDx speaker and a corporate trainer for global companies, now booked almost every week... sometimes twice.
Her book didn't just build awareness; it built a business.

We still laugh about it: we should've charged ten times more.
But like most people starting out, we were charging what *felt* fair instead of what *was* fair.

And then there are authors like May, whose expertise turns their book into an entire consulting ecosystem.

May, the cybersecurity expert, had her book translate complex cybersecurity concepts for small businesses and everyday professionals.
That clarity made her stand out.

Soon she wasn't just selling coaching sessions; she was consulting for multinational corporations across the U.S. and the UAE, commanding six-figure contracts.

Her book didn't just make her visible; it made her *credible.*
She became the go-to authority for cybersecurity for SMEs... and that

credibility still compounds today.

The Founder's Lesson

As I shared earlier in this book, my own publishing journey started with a $65,000 mistake. That experience taught me the hard way that *effort doesn't equal impact.*

It's also what pushed me to master the process, rebuild from scratch, and ultimately design a publishing system that actually works.

So when I talk about pricing from proof—not fear—it comes from experience.

Because when you've seen what a book can create for others and for yourself, you stop undervaluing the transformation it delivers.

The 10× Rule

Today, I apply a simple rule: if what you deliver can help someone earn, save, or create ten times more than they invest, it's not a cost; it's a catalyst.

And the same applies to you.

When your offer delivers real transformation—when it helps someone change their business, career, or life—the only "expensive" thing would be *not* offering it.

Because underpricing doesn't just cheat you.

It cheats the people you serve... by signaling that what you offer isn't as powerful as it truly is.

So stop pricing from fear. Start pricing from proof.

> *When you price with confidence, you give your clients permission to believe in the result.*

Simplify to Amplify

At this point, most authors start getting ideas.

"Maybe I'll build an online course!"
"Or a mastermind!"
"Or a certification program!"
"Or an app!"

Easy there, Picasso.

That's how chaos begins: with good intentions and too many tabs open.

In Step 11, we simplified the system that delivers your message. Now it's time to simplify the offer that monetizes it.

You don't need ten offers or a menu that tries to please everyone. You need one clear offer that delivers one clear transformation.

That's it.

Because when you try to do everything, you dilute your own power.

Look at any successful author-entrepreneur you admire. Chances are, they built their business around one flagship offer—one transformation they became known for—and only *then* added supporting layers around it.

Your book is the entry point.
Your ecosystem connects the dots.
Your offer delivers the transformation.

Everything else is noise until that foundation works.

Think of it like your favorite restaurant. They might have a long menu, but there's *one dish* everyone comes back for... the one they're known for.

That's your job: find your signature dish, perfect it, and serve it consistently.

You can always expand later, but build depth before variety.

Simplifying doesn't mean shrinking your ambition. It means focusing your energy where it matters most... on the offer that drives 80% of your impact and income.

Your ecosystem doesn't need ten doors. It just needs one open one.

Bring It All Home

The irony of scaling is that the more successful you become, the simpler things should get.

You've done the hard work: you wrote the book, built the ecosystem, and designed the offer. Now it's about focus and flow.

Because in the end, scaling isn't about doing more. It's about doing *less*, but better.

Your book planted the seed of trust.

Your ecosystem nurtured the relationship.

Your offers are how you turn that trust into transformation... for your readers *and* for you.

That's the beauty of this stage. You're not just selling a product; you're serving at scale. You're creating pathways for people to grow through your ideas... even when you're not in the room.

And when you realize that, something shifts.

You see that this isn't about "making money from a book."

It's about building a business that keeps delivering value long after someone turns the last page.

So, as we step into the next chapter, it's time to fuel this system.

Because even the best offer can't change lives if nobody sees it.

Next, we'll fuel everything you've built... driving the right traffic into your system so it starts working *for you.*

Welcome to *Step 13 – Fuel the System With Smart Traffic.*

Step 13: Fuel the System With Smart Traffic

Visibility Without Traffic Is a Myth

PICTURE THIS.

An author spends months obsessing over their website. They've got the pixel-perfect logo, a cinematic brand video, a funnel that looks like it was engineered by NASA, and a scheduling link that practically begs to be clicked. Then they post about it once on *Facebook*, get three likes—from their mom, their cousin, and a bot named *CryptoKevin*—and wonder why no one's buying their coaching program.

Their system isn't broken.
It's just deserted.

> *If nobody visits your island, it doesn't matter how beautiful the beach is.*

This is where most authors quietly die inside. They've done the hard part—writing the book, building the offers, setting up the ecosystem—but forget the final step: *getting actual humans to see it*. It's like launching a restaurant and then refusing to put up a sign because "good food should sell itself."

Spoiler: it won't.

Visibility without traffic is a myth.
You can't cash likes. You can't deposit compliments. And no matter how stunning your funnel looks, it won't feed your business until people start walking through the door.

That's why traffic—the *right* traffic—is the energy that keeps your system alive. It doesn't just show up; it powers everything else.
Not random eyeballs, not "maybe someday" followers, but real people already interested in what you offer.

The problem is, most authors think traffic means *getting famous.*
It doesn't. It means *getting found* by the right people, in the right place, at the right time.

The goal isn't vanity metrics; it's meaningful visibility.
Because your book, your offers, and your impact deserve an audience that actually cares... not one that just scrolls.

Why Most Authors Waste Traffic

Let's be honest: most authors don't have a traffic problem.
They have a *wasted traffic* problem.

They'll spend money driving clicks to their website, only to send people to a homepage that says nothing about who it's for or what to do next. Or they'll post motivational quotes on social media every morning, hoping someone—anyone—will magically connect the dots and buy their book.

It's like handing out flyers for your restaurant... with no address printed on them.

Random traffic is noise. Smart traffic is music.

The truth is, not all visitors are created equal. You don't need everyone on the internet; you just need the right ones... the people who actually care about your message, who have the problem you solve, and who are already searching for solutions.

But what do most authors do? They chase volume instead of value.
They obsess over going viral instead of becoming visible to the right audience.
They boost posts that say, *"Check out my new book!"*
instead of *"Here's how to stop wasting hours creating content no one reads."*

Big difference.

Because smart traffic doesn't come from begging for attention; it comes from *earning* relevance.

It's not about inviting everyone to your party; it's about inviting the ones who actually dance.

Before you pour money into ads or collaborations, you need clarity.
Who are you serving?
Where do they hang out?
And what kind of message makes them stop scrolling and say, *"Wait... that's me."*

Otherwise, you're just lighting fireworks in an empty field… loud, expensive, and over in five seconds.

Once you understand that, traffic stops feeling like chaos and starts feeling like control.
You stop chasing clicks and start attracting conversions.
Because you finally know where to show up… and what to say when you do.

The Three Core Traffic Engines

If your author ecosystem is a house, traffic is the electricity.
Without it, everything looks nice, but nothing turns on.

Luckily, there are only three main ways to power your system.
Think of them as your *three core traffic engines*:

- *Organic Authority*

- *Paid Precision*

- *Partnership Power*

You don't need all three running at full blast right away—but when they do, your visibility compounds like interest in a high-yield account.

1. Organic Authority: Build Trust Before the Click

Organic traffic happens when people find you *because* you show up with value, not ads.

It's your podcast interviews, blog posts, SEO articles, and *LinkedIn* thought-leadership content... all the ways you show up as the guide instead of the salesperson.

Organic is slower than paid, but it's more loyal.
Because when someone discovers you through genuine expertise, they trust you *before* they even land on your website.

Take *LinkedIn*, for example. John Nemo built his seven-figure business by starting conversations in the inbox... not selling, not spamming, just connecting.
He calls it the *"money is in the inbox"* principle, because that's where trust turns into business.

Visibility alone doesn't pay the bills. Conversations do.
When someone comments on your post, downloads your free guide, or replies to your email—that's your cue to engage.
Traffic is just the start; the inbox is where you close the loop.

That's what Organic Authority really is: showing up, sharing real value, and turning visibility into genuine conversation.

2. Paid Precision: Speed Meets Strategy

If organic is a garden, paid ads are the greenhouse... they accelerate what's already growing.

Amazon Ads, Meta Ads, and LinkedIn Ads can drive laser-focused traffic when done right.
The key word is *"focused"* because ads don't create demand; they redirect

it.

Here's where most authors mess up: they send cold clicks to a homepage that says nothing about what to do next.

Smart authors send paid traffic to a single next step: a landing page, a free download, a webinar, or even a free chapter from their book.

From there, the conversation shifts to the inbox again.

Whether it's an email nurture sequence or a personal reply from the author, the goal is connection, not just clicks.

Because the real ROI of paid traffic doesn't come from the first sale; it comes from the *second conversation.*

Think of ads not as buying eyeballs, but as *buying time…* a shortcut to start meaningful interactions faster.

3. Partnership Power: Borrow Credibility to Multiply Reach

Partnership Power is how you go from whispering into the void to being introduced to a room full of people who already trust you.

When you collaborate with other authors, influencers, or podcasters who share your audience, you instantly inherit their credibility.

And the best part? Partnership traffic converts faster because it arrives *pre-qualified.*

They already trust the person who sent them your way.

Guest podcast appearances, joint webinars, cross-promotions, or bundled offers… these are low-cost, high-leverage ways to attract the right traffic without spending a dime on ads.

The secret is reciprocity: offer value first. Share your insights, showcase your expertise, and make it a win-win.

Because every collaboration is a trust bridge... and every trust bridge leads to one more email subscriber, one more conversation, and one more client.

4. Your Book Is the Ultimate Traffic Engine

Don't forget the traffic source you already own... *your book.*

Every reader on *Amazon* is a potential lead wandering through your ecosystem without even knowing it. And as you built back in *Step 6,* those CTAs inside your book are the map—quietly guiding readers from curiosity to connection, 24/7 .

That's where your CTAs come in: "Download the free guide," "Join the reader community," or "Take the quiz."
These links quietly turn strangers on *Amazon* into subscribers in your inbox... 24/7, automatically.

It's traffic on autopilot.
Your book keeps working long after launch day, driving warm, pre-sold leads straight into your ecosystem while your inbox keeps doing what it does best: converting relationships into revenue.

When you blend these three engines—your *Organic Authority* keeps you visible, your *Paid Precision* fuels growth, your *Partnership Power* expands reach, and your *Book CTAs* tie it all together—you stop chasing attention and start *owning* it.

That's when your ecosystem finally feels alive.
And the best part? You don't have to hustle harder; you just have to stay connected.

Don't Scale What Doesn't Convert

Before you pour gasoline on your marketing fire, make sure there's actually a spark worth fueling.

Here's the truth: *ads don't fix weak messages; they magnify them.*

If your traffic isn't resonating or your audience targeting is off, no amount of ad spend will fix it... it'll just help you waste money faster.

Most authors make this mistake. They run ads before their house is in order... driving cold clicks to broken pages, vague offers, or CTAs that sound more like chores than opportunities.

It's like turning on a firehose before you've built the pool.

Fix the Flow First

Before you scale, make sure the small stuff works... the CTAs inside your book, your opt-in page, your emails, and that first conversation.
Everything should flow naturally, like a reader being guided from one "aha moment" to the next.

Ask yourself:

- *When someone clicks the link in your book, do they instantly see value or confusion?*

- *When they join your list, do your emails feel personal—or like a robot begging for attention?*

- *When they reply, do you reply back?*

Scaling a broken system just multiplies the noise.
Fix the experience first, then add traffic.

Conversations Before Campaigns

Every sale starts with a conversation.
And every conversation starts because someone felt seen.

That's why John Nemo's *"money is in the inbox"* principle is so powerful...
it reminds you that one-on-one connection still beats any algorithm.
Your ad might start the click, but your inbox finishes the deal.

The best authors don't chase clicks; they build conversations.
They reply to emails, ask follow-up questions, and make their audience feel like part of the story.
Because once someone feels understood, they'll happily move from your free content into your paid world.

Test, Then Turn Up the Volume

When the small version works—the micro tests, the manual follow-ups, the first few paying clients—that's your signal.
Now you can safely scale with confidence.

Because now, every dollar you spend isn't buying *traffic*.

It's buying *proof.*

You've tested your messages in the inbox, refined your offers through real conversations, and seen your CTAs quietly pulling leads from your book every day.
At that point, scaling isn't scary; it's just amplifying what's already working.

So don't throw gasoline on a barbecue that isn't lit yet.
Test the spark. Fix the flame. Then turn up the heat.

Building the Flywheel

At first, traffic feels like pushing a boulder uphill.
You're writing posts, running ads, replying to messages... and wondering if this whole "ecosystem" thing actually works.

But then something shifts.
Momentum.

One channel starts feeding another.
Your book sends readers to your list.
Your list sends people to your offers.
Your offers generate case studies that fuel new content.
Your content attracts partnerships.
And those partnerships send fresh traffic back to your book.

That's when you realize... you've built a *flywheel.*

The Compounding Effect

Smart traffic doesn't move in straight lines; it loops.
A podcast appearance brings a flood of new subscribers who get your emails, click your links, and share your posts.
An ad drives a reader to download your free resource, which triggers your follow-up sequence, which leads them to book a call or buy your course.

Each small action fuels the next.
Each new reader becomes a mini marketing channel of their own—sharing your ideas, quoting your book, and tagging you on LinkedIn.

It's not instant, but it's unstoppable.

Because this kind of momentum doesn't just come from visibility anymore; it comes from synergy. Every part of your system is now feeding the next, turning effort into energy and visibility into velocity.

The Hidden Leverage

When your system is built right, every piece of content, every conversation, and every page of your book becomes part of one living ecosystem.
That's the real magic of authority publishing: everything compounds.

- Your *Organic Authority* keeps bringing in new people who already trust you.

- Your *Paid Precision* lets you scale what's working without guessing.

- Your *Partnership Power* expands your reach into new audiences.

- Your *Book CTAs* quietly turn Amazon readers into subscribers every day.

- And your *Inbox Conversations* convert curiosity into clients.

It's all connected.

Each piece amplifies the others... until your business runs on momentum, not muscle.

When the System Feeds Itself

That's when you finally graduate from *hustling for traffic* to *owning attention.*

You wake up to new subscribers, new clients, and new messages from readers who found you through a podcast you did months ago.

And the best part? It's sustainable.

Because you're no longer dependent on one ad, one launch, or one platform.

You've built an ecosystem that fuels itself... a flywheel that keeps spinning long after you stop pushing.

That's not luck.

That's leverage.

> *Momentum doesn't come from working harder. It comes from building systems that keep working when you're not.*

Now that your system is fueled, it's time to turn it into something bigger... something that powers your entire business.

From Traffic to Momentum

At this point, you've done what most authors never do.

You didn't just write a book; you built an engine. And now, you've learned how to fuel it.

You've gone from chasing attention to creating predictable visibility. From "posting and praying" to knowing exactly how to attract, capture, and convert the right audience... again and again.

And the best part?

It's not luck. It's leverage.

Your *Organic Authority* plants the seeds.

Your *Paid Precision* accelerates growth.

Your *Partnership Power* multiplies reach.

Your *Book CTAs* quietly bring readers into your world.

Your *Inbox Conversations* turn strangers into clients—and clients into fans.

That's not marketing.

That's momentum... the kind that compounds without burning you out.

Because smart traffic isn't about doing more.

It's about connecting the dots between everything you've already built.

Your book, your ecosystem, and your offers... they're not separate projects anymore.

They're parts of one living machine that runs on trust, attention, and conversation.

And once that flywheel starts spinning, it doesn't stop.

You've built the system. You've fueled it. Now it's time to scale it.

In the next chapter, we'll take everything you've built—the book, the ecosystem, the offers, and the traffic—and show you how to turn it into a *Business Growth Engine.*

A system that doesn't just move; it scales. One that keeps working whether you're writing, resting, or enjoying that well-earned coffee somewhere warm.

Publishing a book was never the endgame.

It was the spark that ignited everything else.

Step 14: Turn Your Book Into a Business Growth Engine

From System to Engine

ONCE YOUR SYSTEM STARTS running, a new choice appears.

Some authors keep driving manually... working harder, polishing every part, and hoping effort alone keeps things moving.
Others step back, plug in the engine, and let their business start running on its own.

Guess which one's smiling on a Tuesday afternoon while sipping an iced coffee somewhere sunny?

Here's the thing: a car with the engine off still looks impressive, but it's not going anywhere.

The same goes for your author ecosystem.

You've already done the heavy lifting... you wrote the book, built the funnel, and designed offers that serve your readers. But if everything depends on you showing up every single day, you don't have a business. You have a very busy job... with a boss who's impossible to quit.

This final step isn't just about transforming your book; it's about transforming *you.*

You're not just an author anymore. You're an entrepreneur with an engine.

The difference? Entrepreneurs build systems that keep working even when they step away. Authors in manual mode don't.

And once you turn on that engine—through automation, delegation, and optimization—everything you've built starts compounding. Leads keep coming in. Readers keep discovering you. Clients keep enrolling.

Even when you're offline.

Because the real magic of *Publish, Promote, Monetize* isn't that you can sell books.
It's that you can stop selling your time.

Ready to turn the key?

Why Most Authors Stay Stuck in Manual Mode

Most authors stay stuck in *manual mode...* the exhausting, never-ending loop of doing everything themselves.

They post, comment, and message like their book's life depends on it. They refresh their inbox 47 times a day. Every new lead feels like a win... until it creates another task.

Manual mode *looks* productive because it's busy. You can see the gears turning: emails going out, posts getting likes, and invoices being sent. But it's motion, not momentum.

You can't out-hustle broken systems.

At some point, every author hits the same wall: *the bottleneck is you.*

I know because I've lived it.

When I first started *Authority Publishing*, I was the bottleneck. Everything ran through me… every call, every plan, every ad tweak. I was proud of how much I could juggle until I realized I was also quietly slowing things down.

There were times I turned down marketing opportunities without even realizing it… because deep down, I knew I couldn't handle more clients. So I'd pause campaigns, telling myself I was "staying focused," only to create my own ceiling.

Then, when I finally had time again, I'd double down—generate new leads, fill the pipeline—and hit the same wall weeks later.

That cycle repeated until I made one critical decision: stop doing everything myself.

I built systems and leveraged other people's time, skills, and expertise. I trained them to deliver with the same care and embody the same values. And that's when everything changed.

Suddenly, I wasn't the engine anymore; I was the architect.

That's when *Authority Publishing* truly started to scale. Not because I worked harder, but because I finally let go.

And that's exactly where you are right now.

You've built something worth scaling. The next step is to *free it…* by automating what can be automated and delegating what others can do just as well (or better) than you.

Let's start there.

Automate the Essentials

Here's the good news: not everything in your business needs your fingerprints.

Some tasks should run like clockwork... predictable, repeatable, and invisible. These are your *automation candidates*: the quiet parts that keep the engine running smoothly while you focus on what only you can do.

Think of automation as cloning your best self... minus the caffeine addiction and 2 a.m. replies.

It's not about removing the human touch; it's about multiplying it. Automation ensures your readers, leads, and clients are cared for consistently, even when you're offline.

Here's where to start:

1. ***Email Nurture Sequences.***
   Your email list is the core of your ecosystem... the place every reader connection begins. But you can't personally follow up with every new reader... and you shouldn't try.

   Automation lets you build trust on autopilot. You can guide readers through a series of friendly, value-packed messages that educate, entertain, and invite them to take the next step... whether that's booking a call, joining a program, or downloading another resource.

Each message strengthens the relationship while you sleep.

2. ***Evergreen Funnels,***
   Instead of launching over and over, create *evergreen pathways* that convert readers into leads—and leads into clients—all year long.

   Your book might lead to a free training, that training leads to a call, and that call leads to your offer... all without you lifting a finger after setup.

   Same work as a live launch, but it keeps running every day.

3. ***Lead Capture & Follow-Up Systems.***
   Set up simple forms and automations that tag new leads, send follow-ups, and notify you (or your team) when someone engages.

   It's your digital concierge... welcoming new readers, introducing them to your world, and gently guiding them toward your higher-value offers.

4. ***Onboarding Workflows.***
   Once a client joins, your system should automatically welcome them, send materials, and deliver what they paid for... without you scrambling to send links or reminders.

   Everything happens seamlessly, from payment to delivery.

When I finally automated these essentials at *Authority Publishing*, something remarkable happened.

Calls got booked while I slept. Clients onboarded themselves. And for the first time, I felt the freedom I'd been promising others.

That's when I understood what leverage really means... *doing the work once and letting it keep working for you.*

As author and entrepreneur Chandler Bolt calls it, *Leveraged Impact*: the effort you invest once continues to generate results long after you've moved on.

So don't think of automation as robotic. Think of it as the quiet heartbeat of your business... the rhythm that keeps everything alive, even when you're away.

Up next, let's talk about how to *delegate for growth...* because even with automation, no system scales without people.

Delegate for Growth

You can't scale while clinging to control.

Most authors—especially the perfectionist kind—struggle with delegation. We tell ourselves no one can do it as well as we do. That it's "faster if I just do it myself." That our work is too specialized to outsource.

That's how we stay trapped.

I was there. Even after automating the systems at *Authority Publishing*, everything still ran through me. Every client call, every campaign, every ad review. Until I admitted that my obsession with quality had quietly turned into *fear*... fear of letting go.

So I stopped trying to be Superman and started building a team.

At first, it felt strange... like handing your newborn to someone else. But with the right people, training, and processes, the results didn't just match mine; they surpassed them.

I began with simple, repeatable tasks: scheduling, admin, and inbox management. Then design, ads, and client communication. The turning point came when I saw my team start making decisions using the same logic I would.

That's when I stopped managing and started multiplying.

Delegation isn't about cloning yourself; it's about multiplying your impact.

You hire designers so your book looks professional without you learning *Photoshop*.
You hire editors so your manuscript reads clean without you proofreading for hours.
You hire assistants so your calendar stays sane while you focus on creating.

Every minute you buy back compounds your freedom and focus.

When I finally stepped out of the weeds, *Authority Publishing* started to grow... not in chaos, but in rhythm. Launches became smoother. Response times faster. Authors happier. And me? I got my time—and my sanity—back.

Truth is, I couldn't have dedicated weeks—sometimes months—to writing this very book if I hadn't automated, delegated, and built a team I trust.

That's the real ROI of delegation: not just profit, but peace. The space to think, to create, to lead.

Because once your systems run and your people perform, you stop *working in* the business... and start *building on* it.

Next, let's talk about how to *leverage what already works*—the secret to multiplying results without multiplying effort.

Leverage What Already Works

Here's the beautiful part about reaching this stage: *you don't need to reinvent anything.*

Your book, offers, and ecosystem have already shown you what works. You've tested ideas, watched what resonates, and seen what actually moves people to action. The next level isn't about adding more; it's about doing more with what's already working.

When most authors hit a plateau, their instinct is to create something new... a new course, a new funnel, or a new book. But what they really need is to *double down* on what's already delivering results.

Because leverage isn't about starting over. It's about squeezing every ounce of value from what you've already built.

Here's how that looks in practice:

- If a webinar converted well once, record it and make it evergreen.

- If a podcast interview brought in leads, turn the best clips into social posts or short videos.

- If one chapter of your book sparked messages or client inquiries, expand it into a keynote or workshop.

Every piece of content, every call, and every conversation can be multiplied when you treat it like an *asset* instead of a one-time effort.

I've seen this play out at *Authority Publishing* countless times. One of our authors hosted a small live workshop that converted better than any ad campaign we'd run. Instead of chasing the next big idea, we refined it, recorded it, and built it into an automated webinar funnel. That single workshop kept generating leads for months while she moved on to her next book.

Another author's post-launch video exploded organically. Rather than create something new, we edited that same video into short reels, added it to her landing page, and turned it into a mini ad campaign. Same message. Ten times the reach.

That's the compounding power of leverage.

And the truth is, your single biggest advantage in today's marketplace is *you:* your story, your personality, and your authentic voice.

So stop hiding it behind one platform or one format. Let it echo across every touchpoint in your ecosystem.

Your book isn't just one product; it's a library of insights and stories that can be repurposed endlessly to open new doors into your world.

Leverage means you've stopped chasing opportunities and started *engineering* them.

And once you've identified what works and multiplied it, the next step is simple: measure, refine, and repeat... the rhythm behind every scalable business engine.

Measure, Refine, and Multiply

If automation is the heartbeat and delegation is the muscle, then measurement is the nervous system of your business engine.

Without it, you're just guessing... hoping your book, funnel, or ads are "probably" working. But hope isn't a growth strategy. Data is.

Smart authors treat numbers like signposts. Each click, open, and conversion tells a story about what your audience values most.

When I started looking closely at *Authority Publishing's* metrics—ad performance, booking rates, and conversion data—I realized growth was never about doing *more*. It was about doing *better*.

A few small tweaks often outperformed big overhauls.
Changing one word in a headline boosted clicks.
Moving a testimonial higher on a page doubled conversions.
Simplifying a lead magnet made more people sign up.

That's when it clicked: sustainable growth isn't about guessing what will work next; it's about listening to what's already speaking through the numbers.

So, what should you measure?

- ***Conversion rates:*** How many visitors actually take action?

- ***Email engagement:*** Which stories and subject lines get the most clicks?

- ***Ad performance:*** Which audiences bring the best return?

- ***Reader behavior:*** Where do people drop off in your funnel, and where do they stay?

The data doesn't just tell you what's working; it tells you *why.*

And once you understand that, refinement becomes your superpower.

The best engines aren't built once; they're tuned regularly.

> *Each month, take what's working and make it 10% better.*
> *Update your book description. Test a new ad headline. Refresh your email subject lines.*
> *Those small, steady improvements compound like interest.*

That's how you multiply impact without multiplying effort.

At *Authority Publishing*, this approach turned steady growth into exponential results. We stopped guessing, started measuring, refined what worked, and kept multiplying it. Each improvement—no matter how small—added horsepower to the engine.

Before long, the system that once felt fragile started running like a machine.

And that's what I want for you.

Because when your book, your ecosystem, and your offers all feed one another, you stop wondering where the next client or reader will come from.

The engine runs. The impact grows.
And the business keeps scaling... with or without you.

From Book to Engine, From Author to Architect

Look back at the road you've built.

You started this journey with a message... something you knew the world needed to hear. You learned how to publish with purpose, promote with strategy, and monetize with integrity.

But here's the truth: you didn't just build a book. You built an *engine*.

Your words became a brand.

Your readers became relationships.

Your systems became a business that grows even when you're not pushing the pedal.

And that's the point of it all... *to create something that keeps moving without you constantly driving it.*

Because the real reward of becoming an authority isn't about more sales, followers, or speaking gigs; it's about freedom.

The freedom to create on your own terms, to focus on the ideas that matter, and to actually live the message your book set in motion.

I know because I've lived it. *Authority Publishing* started as me doing everything myself... and it grew into a company that runs on systems, trust, and a team that shares my vision.

That's what this entire journey has been about: moving from operator to architect, from author to entrepreneur, from book to business.

So as you turn the page to the conclusion, remember this:

Your book isn't the end of your story. It's the start of your next one.

The systems are running.

The engine is alive.

And the road ahead? Wide open.

Conclusion

Every author knows that strange mix of relief and nostalgia when you finish a book. The typing stops, the drafts end, and you finally lean back with that quiet thought... *I did it.*

But here's what most people don't realize: publishing your book isn't the finish line. It's the starting line of your next chapter.

Think of your book as the ignition key in a brand-new engine. You've spent the last several chapters learning how to build it piece by piece — *Publish, Promote, Monetize.* Now it's time to turn the key and hear it roar. That sound? That's the hum of momentum, credibility, and opportunity working together.

When you started this journey, your dream was simple: to share your story, your message, or your expertise. Along the way, you discovered that books aren't just stories; they're systems. You learned how to position your book with precision, promote it with intention, and monetize it with purpose.

You didn't just become an author. You became an authority. You built more than a book; you built a business engine that can grow while you sleep, nurture relationships while you work, and attract opportunities you never thought possible.

The real win isn't about book sales or rankings. It's about freedom. It's waking up to a calendar filled with discovery calls from readers who already trust you because of your book. It's opening your inbox to invitations, collaborations, and partnerships... all because you built something that speaks for you.

Success isn't the number of copies you sell. It's the number of lives your message touches
and the number of doors it opens for your future.

You've built your foundation. You've seen how each step connects: the book, the ecosystem, the offers, and the traffic. Now it's time to keep refining, evolving, and expanding your reach.

If this book leaves you with one takeaway, let it be this: you don't have to do the next phase alone. You've already proven your commitment by getting this far. The next level is about leverage... using your systems, your audience, and your time more effectively.

At *Authority Publishing*, that's what we help authors do: scale their impact, automate their growth, and keep their message alive long after launch day. We're here when you're ready to turn your book into a full-scale business engine.

So take a moment to appreciate how far you've come. You've published your book, built your brand, and learned to monetize your message. Now it's time to keep the momentum going... to build the business, the lifestyle, and the legacy your book was meant to create.

The pages you've just read aren't the end of your story. They're the beginning of everything you've been preparing for.

Your next chapter isn't waiting to be written. It's waiting to be lived.

Help Me Help Other Authors

IF YOU'VE MADE IT this far—thank you.

Truly. Writing this book was a journey, and the fact that you've stayed with me through every page means the world.

If this book helped you—even in one small way—would you take a minute to leave a quick review on *Amazon*?

Your honest words (even a single sentence!) make a real difference. They help more authors, coaches, and consultants like you discover this book, learn the system, and finally share their own message with the world.

Just head over to Amazon, click *Write a Customer Review*, and share what you found most valuable. It doesn't have to be long—a few genuine words can go a long way.

https://www.amazon.com/Publish-Promote-Monetize-Authority-Perso nal-ebook/dp/B0GQJ3WJL6

By sharing your experience, you're not just supporting this book; you're helping other author-entrepreneurs publish with purpose, promote with confidence, and monetize with integrity.

Your review could be the nudge someone needs to finally start writ-

ing their book... and change their life.

About H.J. Chammas

If you'd told H.J. Chammas years ago that losing $65,000 on his first book would become the best thing that ever happened to him, he probably would've laughed—nervously.

Back then, he was like most first-time authors: excited, hopeful, and completely unaware that the publishing world had a few hard lessons in store. He poured his heart (and savings) into a deal with a "big-name" self-publishing company that promised the world: wide distribution, marketing support, and a shot at bestseller status. What he got instead was silence, disappointment, and a royalty check that barely covered a cup of coffee.

That failure could've been the end of his author dream. Instead, it became his awakening.

Determined to figure out what went wrong, H.J. rolled up his sleeves and learned everything the hard way... keywords, categories, metadata, cover psychology, ad optimization, and reader behavior. He republished his book on his own terms, retitled and repositioned it, and within months it climbed the charts to become a bestseller. Then he did it again. And again. And again.

Over time, *The Employee Millionaire* series became an international success, and H.J. became a four-time bestselling author... not by luck, but by mastering the system behind the success.

When other authors started asking how he did it, he shared his process freely... helping them fix their listings, relaunch their books, and build authority in their niches. Every single one of them hit bestseller status. That's when H.J. realized this wasn't just a personal victory. It was a repeatable framework.

That framework became *Authority Publishing*: a company built to help experts, coaches, and consultants publish, promote, and monetize their books the right way. No vanity promises. No smoke and mirrors. Just real systems that turn books into business growth engines.

Today, *Authority Publishing* has helped over 50 authors achieve bestseller success—many of whom went on to build thriving businesses, attract clients, and expand their impact through their books.

H.J. often says, *"Don't sell the book—sell what the book sells."* And he lives by that. His own books have opened doors to speaking engagements, consulting opportunities, and a global network of readers who became clients and collaborators.

When he's not teaching authors how to build authority through publishing, H.J. is a husband, a dad, and a firm believer that the real ROI of a book isn't measured in royalties; it's measured in the lives it changes, including your own.

Your next chapter starts now.

www.authority-publishing.com

Acknowledgements

To my team: thank you for helping me turn this vision into something real. None of this would exist without your talent, your trust, and your relentless belief in our mission.

And to my wife, Joyce: thank you for believing in me when I failed, especially after I spent 18 months writing my first book only to see it flop. You could have told me to give up. Instead, you reminded me who I am and pushed me to try again. That faith became the seed of everything I've built since... from rebuilding that first book to creating *Authority Publishing* and, ultimately, this system that now helps others do the same.

You saw the author, the entrepreneur, and the dreamer long before anyone else did.

This one's for you.